Black Bag to Blackberry®

A MAINE PEDIATRICIAN'S 40-YEAR JOURNEY

By Conner M. Moore, M.D.

Black Bag to Blackberry®
A Maine Pediatrician's 40-Year Journey

Published by Bryson Taylor Publishing
ISBN 978-0-9841934-3-1
LOC PCN 2010940561

Written by Conner M. Moore, M.D.

Cover Art by Jasmin Demers
Graphic Designer Donna Berger
Edited by Michael Moore & Bryson Taylor Publishing

Bryson Taylor Publishing
199 New County Road
Saco, Maine 04072
www.brysontaylorpublishing.com

BRYSON
TAYLOR
PUBLISHING

To Wendy,

With love and thanks

A special acknowledgement and thanks to a very brave young lady, Jessi whose last wish was that she be remembered for her courage and grit.

In her name, we have started a non-profit foundation, Jessi's Gift. Proceeds from this book will be donated to Jessi's Gift to support nursing scholarships.

Your tax-deductible donations can be sent to:

Jessi's Gift, P.O. Box 1234, Biddeford, Maine 04005

CHAPTERS

PART I

PART II

PART III

PREFACE

While attending a Boston workshop for aspiring medical writers, I learned that every other caregiver in America is writing a memoir. Many have powerful stories, others are pounding out *Recovering from the Heartbreak of Hangnail Surgery.* What differentiates me?

I have enjoyed telling stories, and after almost a quarter million office visits with children and their families, I've got quite a few. The timing of my career positioned me to watch the advent of powerful drugs and vaccines, advances in medical technology, the rise of malpractice lawsuits, and changes in the delivery of health care and small town America.

Many doctor's biographies are often told in fictionalized form with the names of the patients changed. Almost to a person, parents and children have given me permission to use their names, and their trust has been very humbling. "We would be honored, Dr. Moore," said one mother. In these days of bad news, I have tried to inject humor into these chapters.

What I don't bring to this book is judgment. If I have learned anything from all of this doctoring, it is that you just never know what someone else has gone through or what their present circumstance is. When I glance into my waiting room and see a teen with a Mohawk and the wife of a CEO, chatting to each other while holding new babies, I know that my office and my staff foster this idea.

I want to briefly thank my son Michael for editing this book. Wendy started referring to him as "Slash" about halfway through this project. He has gently culled my bad metaphors, lame jokes and inappropriate meanderings. My favorite was the deletion of a rambling disquisition on my distaste for flavored coffee with a stern explanation that "you are better than this." His requests to "please explain" or "redo entirely" were plentiful, but seeing passages marked "gem" or "weepy" gave me the energy to carry on.

Lastly, there are my heroes. They are the nurses and other caregivers who arrive through blizzards and floods, on nights and weekends, to the hospital and office to heal children. They are the parents of chronically ill children who struggle through countless appointments, mountains of insurance forms, and all-nighters of illness and tears – never giving up. And finally, there are the brave children with chronic conditions – the ones with missing limbs, colostomies, wheezing lungs, and wheelchairs. Come and meet them.

Taking the lead from the Romans, my book is also divided into three parts. The first section roughly describes events during my first eleven years in small group practice, followed by stories from my next seventeen years in solo practice, ending with tales from twelve years of corporate medicine – until my retirement in 2008. I have taken a few liberties with the chronology to push some child stories forward.

My first office was attached to my senior partner's house in historical Saco, Maine. The next solo office was a converted snowmobile shop adjacent to our new hospital – both constructed in 1979. Several months before retirement, I relocated to a new modern medical office building.

My children would agree that a separate book could be written regarding the former snowmobile (Rupp) store AKA Ruppshop.

Dr. Conner M. Moore

INTRODUCTION

In 1956, a week after graduating from high school, I nervously circled our family car around a suburban residential block and finally knocked at a modest house. After a few moments the door opened and, although we had never met, a middle-aged couple embraced me. They had awarded me scholarship money in honor of their only child John, who had had succumbed to polio early in his senior year. The funds had been earmarked for John's college tuition.

Two years later, I sat for my final exam in organic chemistry. This mandatory pre-med course is the dreaded five hundred pound gorilla that guards the door to medical school. Failure to wrestle this beast to the ground annually redirects thousands of wannabe doctors to the greener pastures of English, sociology, or history.

We were handed a single page exam, and a communal groan echoed throughout the vast gymnasium. The innocent sheet asked only two questions. The more challenging exercise posed this query; *This is the chemical formula for chloramphenicol, a new antibiotic. Please make it from scratch.* Hadn't Parke Davis already spent millions to engineer these chemical reactions? Several students arose and silently exited the building.

Although my humanities grades were rarely better than the proverbial gentleman's C, chemical compounding was my forte. A brew of carbon, hydrogen and chlorine appeared effortlessly on the pages of my blue book. "Damn I'm good," I whispered. An A in organic chemistry counteracted a disaster in Advanced Spanish and paved the way to medical school.

After medical school, I spent a year interning at Boston City Hospital. During this time, I met Wendy through a mutual friend. She had left Montreal to take a nursing position at Children's Hospital. My new Canadian acquaintance would sometimes grumble about getting along with pediatricians; I, the young internist, would agree - they weren't real physicians. Little did we know then that Wendy would soon become my partner for life and the mother of our three sons while I would morph into a baby doctor. Her help, support, and love over forty years would make my pediatric career possible.

The Air Force beckoned next. I could spend two years with the pediatricians and obstetricians, or become a general medical officer doing routine physicals from nine to five. I selected the former and was soon ready for pediatric residency. Several prestigious hospitals were not willing to give me credit for my military experience, but the Cincinnati Children's Hospital welcomed me.

After a busy two years in the sweltering heat of the Midwest it was time for a move. In the summer of 1968, Wendy and my first son Christopher traveled to stay with her parents in Canada because of civil unrest in Cincinnati. I remained to finish my training. The plan was to meet up in Saco, Maine, where I would be joining Dr. Maurice Ross. I would be the first new physician in the area in eleven years.

Fellow residents were politely aghast at my career choices - general pediatrics was bad enough, but doing it in Maine would be compounding the error. Many of my peers pursued academic careers in pediatric specialties and had to change hospitals every few years. But, forty-one years later, I am writing this from my kitchen table in Saco.

Dr. Ross had been practicing pediatrics in his hometown since 1947. The vast majority of the Maine pediatricians toiled in solo practice while frantically searching for partners. Dr. Ross and I would be the only pediatricians in York County. As was common practice, the office was actually part of his house.

Northern York County begins with seven miles of sandy beach arising from the cold Atlantic. The land stretches into miles of sloping farmland, then north to densely pined foothills and eventually to the granite peaks of the New Hampshire and western Maine White Mountains. This geography may dictate family occupations of fisherperson, farmer, or lumberman. Seaweed, cow manure, or sawdust might be tracked onto the office carpet.

Within days I would be mixing a vial of *chloramphenicol* antibiotic to save the life of an infant with meningitis and administering polio vaccine, unavailable to my deceased high school classmate, John.

OFF TO WORK WE GO

In 1968, we were busy. The birth of the Medicaid program assured us a steady stream of outpatient children, and it was not unusual to examine forty to fifty a day. My personal best was eighty-three children in twelve hours one day when Dr. Ross was on vacation. I say this not to brag, but to communicate the reality we were facing. We would dictate aloud to the nurses as we examined each child, a practice that would hardly fly with today's HIPPA regulations. They would then enter the information longhand into the chart, write any prescriptions, and give verbal instructions to the parents. It was not an ideal system but served both doctors and families fairly well. We soon upgraded to mini-cassettes and transcriptionists.

Insurance did not cover office visits. At the time these visits cost the same as a hundred first class stamps. Six dollars, six cents. This formula held true for many years until medical costs skyrocketed. We never refused to see a sick child regardless of the family's ability to pay, and Medicaid children comprised roughly one-third of the practice. Regardless of one's political position it must be said that the Medicaid program fostered timely visits to the doctor for routine care and illness. Children with severe illness no longer appeared in the emergency room late on a Saturday night. The state reimbursement paid our overhead for each child, but there was not much left over for the doctor. We considered this service to be a gift back to the community.

I would soon be faced with all manner of sick children –

the unknowingly pregnant teen who arrived for a sports physical, the siblings with carbon monoxide poisoning, and the child who was biting down vigorously on my finger each time I flipped the sphere of hard candy up off his larynx.

Here's what we didn't have in 1968 - emergency room doctors, intensive care units, ventilators for newborns, pediatric surgeons, pediatric specialists, and transport service. Thus, I was forced to administer chemotherapy, give allergy shots, do stitches, stabilize basic fractures, and occasionally assist with surgery. While cutting and tying sutures in a child's abdomen, my only wish was that the chief surgeon not have his own medical emergency.

All of this led to wildly unpredictable working hours. Whenever I called home to check in regarding yet another late night, Wendy, with typical patience and grace, would understand what we had signed up for and wind down the conversation with, "well, your dinner's on the hot tray." In the background my children would snicker at the predictability of this dialog. When I finally got home, the dinner that Wendy had lovingly prepared would be somewhat reduced in size after an evening on the hot tray. At midnight, these meals showed wear but were still delicious. If I crawled in at six in the morning, they were fully desiccated.

I learned that I would need a keen sense of humor and wonderment. You need to know the parent's occupation and the child's hobbies and sports interests, preferably without glancing at their office chart. Special attention must be paid to any gift a child offers you, be it a drawing, a Popsicle-stick house, or a rock. Days off were not really off. There always seemed to be emergency Cesarean sections or exchange transfusions. My vacations were restorative, but when I returned from them my partner would immediately take off for his ten days of rest and relaxation.

In the subsequent chapters, I will attempt to paint a picture of small town pediatrics, from house calls to phone calls, footballs to snowballs, and a few very personal chapters about beautiful and courageous families. Please join me.

**Pictured: 372 Main Street Saco; Dr. Ross's home
and our office Photo taken: 2010**

MAINE: THE WAY LIFE SHOULD BE

"Maine - The Way Life Should Be." That's what the sign says as you cross over the border heading north on I-95. It is an absurd marketing slogan, presumptuous and even contentious. But there may be a hint of truth to the phrase.

It was just after Christmas in 1970 when I picked up the chart of a sick child. The patient in question was the youngster of an all-summer vacationing family from the Boston suburbs. I started to ask father whom they were visiting for the holidays. Then the local address became evident. During the past August father had been in the office frequently. His children had poison ivy, sunburn, and all the other usual summer maladies. At each visit he would engage in an extended rant about the city and the suburbs, the commuting and the cost.

Finally one day I said, "If you really don't like it there, then quit your job and move here". My friend mumbled and walked away.

Six months later he was more talkative. "Funny thing, Doc. Last time I talked with you I was having a hard time thinking about my family's future. Couldn't sleep at night. Couldn't decide. So I quit my job and moved the family to Old Orchard Beach and got a new job. Doesn't pay as much, but we don't need as much. The whole family's happy. Thanks, neighbor."

"Oh yeah," he finished. "If it hadn't worked out, it would have been your fault."

Right about that time, our local school was auctioning off old furniture from the former headmaster's home. Our eye was on an antique square walnut table which sat four. Having sparse money remaining from residency, Wendy and I were quickly outbid by a local antique dealer.

My senior partner's wife suggested that we go chat with the winning bidder and see if we could broker a deal. We all trooped a few miles south. The owner seemed friendly and approachable. Although I seldom introduce myself as a doctor, I broke the rule and played the "new doctor" card. It seemed to work.

"Well Doc, the van is coming from Missouri to pick up this lot. If you can pay me the price on the tag and get it out of the barn before the truck comes – she's yours."

Suddenly the price seemed more reasonable.

"Deal", I quickly responded.

He started to walk away. Then he turned.

"You know Doc, this table was made in Boston. I think I have parts from a sister table up in the loft."

Yes indeed. Upstairs we found five more leaves that fit our table. We also found ten more chairs.

"I'll throw these in. I had forgotten about them. No use without a table and I already made the deal with you."

We headed back north with table parts lashed all over our station wagon. We could now seat fourteen, at no extra charge.

Although our county is becoming less semi-rural and more suburban, there still are practice families where the breadwinner is a lumberjack, farmer or fisherman. My favorite was the goat lady from Kennebunk. Goat fragrance cannot be mistaken for anything else, and I always knew when this family had arrived. Sadly this family found Maine becoming too crowded and they moved to Nova Scotia. Before E-Z Pass I had several mothers in my practice who were toll collectors for the Maine Turnpike Authority. It was not unusual for them to stick their heads into our fully loaded family car as it reentered Maine. "Hi Doc. Welcome back to Maine. Looks like you've been on vacation."

Our friend Denise owns a local seafood restaurant right on the ocean. Last year she called me during the afternoon on a September Sunday. "Hey Dr. Moore. You've got a six o'clock reservation. We're running low on haddock and I just wanted you to start thinking about a second choice before you come."

During one of our many recessions I needed to refinance my office building to raise some cash for daily expenses. During lean times families often couldn't pay doctor bills. The big banks had no bargains but a local banker provided a very low refinance rate with no appraisal fee. He knew my practice was heavily Medicaid(ed) and served the poor. He wanted to say thank you.

7

Finally, if you live in certain rural areas, the State of Maine will monitor your property from a surveillance aircraft while you are away. It's a free service. The only downside is the plane will also scan your garden and your shrubbery. And, as a startled mother in my practice discovered, an eagle-eyed Drug Enforcement Agency pilot might just misidentify the beautiful cosmos flowers in your garden for marijuana plants. It's an honest mistake, and after a visit from the police, you might even get an apology.

Pictured: The Original Walnut Table now in Christopher's house in Colorado

JESSI

"I don't know, Dr. Moore. Jessica just isn't gaining any weight." With this plea from Jessi's mother Joanne, we all embarked upon a twelve-year odyssey of pain, laughter, and tears.

In the beginning, I hoped that three-month-old Jessi's condition was due to troubles with breast-feeding. But this was naive and when I found out that she had two relatives with cystic fibrosis, the die was cast. Jessi was evaluated in Boston, where after some delay, she was diagnosed with cystic fibrosis. With formula feedings and pancreatic replacement powder, she thrived. I told her parents that there would be plenty of challenges ahead.

Jessi was hospitalized at age three with pneumonia. Cultures demonstrated that she was colonized with pseudomonas bacteria, a common finding for children with cystic fibrosis. This chronic disease, like asthma, can cause life-threatening pneumonia during infancy or just mild bronchitis later in life. Current research suggests that certain gene markers may predict the severity of the disease. Another child with cystic fibrosis in my practice showed just a bland strain of staph. He had only one bout of pneumonia during his childhood.

Jessi's days began to take on a routine of inhalations, physical therapy, and oral medications. Initially Jessi was followed in the cystic fibrosis clinic in our medical center. But, in my opinion, she was being undertreated. The job of quarterbacking her illness fell to me by default.

9

The late Dr. Sydney Gellis, a renowned Boston pediatrician, used to say that while kids with leukemia felt well during remission, children with cystic fibrosis, even on good days, still felt lousy. Talking with experts around New England, we tried new medicines and nebulizer treatments. Some of the exotic remedies were obtained from special pharmacies in Massachusetts and Canada.

Jessi started school. She tired easily and was admitted to the hospital more frequently. Dr. Atul Gawande, a surgeon and bestselling medical writer, investigated why cystic fibrosis patients at the University of Minnesota lived ten years longer than their counterparts elsewhere. The answer was complex but the winning ticket was meticulous attention to detail. Even a slight decrease in lung function would trigger an admission to the ward for a "clean out". Children were placed in vibrating pulmonary jackets at an early age. Missed clinic visits were not tolerated. The list went on and on. Today, I might have suggested that Jessi and her family move to Minnesota.

We lacked many of the newer tools available today - pulse oximeters to measure oxygen levels and the C reactive protein blood test to screen for infections. Controversy raged around the efficacies of new treatments. You had to pick and choose. At age six Jessi dropped to twenty-six pounds. Her malnutrition was due to a combination of poor appetite, fever and the simple progression of her disease. Today cystic fibrosis children, like baseball players, are being treated with human growth hormone and anabolic steroids to stabilize weight and increase muscle mass.

10

At lunch, during a conference in Phoenix, a pulmonary expert from Tucson gave it to me straight.

"You do know, Dr. Moore, that if you don't place a feeding gastrostomy soon, Jessi is going to die."

He then related stories of adults with this disease, who gained thirty pounds after the procedure and went back to work. The gastrostomy creates a half inch round window between the stomach and skin in the left upper abdomen. A "button" is then placed in the window. Liquid feedings, with imaginary flavors, could be dripped in through the button overnight. We did this for Jessi, and a few years later we placed a Port-a-Cath over her right anterior chest to connect to a large internal chest vein. We now had permanent vein access. Caring for Jessi's catheters and tubing earned me a degree in medical plumbing.

But this story is not about the nuts and bolt of treating cystic fibrosis. Wendy cared for a number of children with cystic fibrosis during her time at Boston Children's Hospital. She has commented that these and other chronically ill children have wisdom beyond their years. They ask questions about life which we often cannot answer. They instantly focus you away from the material and petty. Jessi was the poster child for all the above.

Jessi always had the same hospital room. With approval from middle management it had been wallpapered with her favorite pattern, and her name was on the door. Visitors and parents of new admissions would stare in shock as they peeked through the door into her room.

It looked like a blend of Chuck E Cheese and the Cumberland County Fair.

Monday night was always "gotcha" night. Jessi would dress up in costume, often scary, and spook her doctor and other hospital personnel. One night we attempted a difficult trick from a magic book and got raw egg everywhere. Jessi loved to pour fake green slime onto her pediatrician and into his medical bag. A physician can't seem too snobbish when he looks like he has just stepped off a Three Stooges set. Years later, when I greet nurses on the street, they still vividly remember these little one act plays.

One Halloween Jessi dressed as a troll and I dressed as a pirate. We went to a local production of *Little Shop of Horrors*. Our favorite annual event was to ride with Santa on his lobster boat into Kennebunkport Harbor to help distribute gifts to the waiting children.

Jessi was always roaming around the hospital in-between her treatments. The hospital should have rebated her insurance company for missed meals and unslept-in beds. There was a fifty-fifty chance of finding her when making rounds. Jessi did many routine tasks for the nurses and had her own Florence Nightingale cap and nametag. She felt that she was owed an associate degree.

Jessi was a huge fan of the boy band New Kids on the Block. One evening we fibbed and told Jessi that she was receiving an overnight pass for a sleepover at her aunt's house.

As we stood in front of the hospital, a stretch limo rolled up and the door opened.

"What's this?" She demanded.

"Get in", we answered. Jessi screamed as the limo departed for a concert in Old Orchard Beach.

Despite the red tape surrounding supplemental airline oxygen, Jessi made it to Disney World, courtesy of the Starlight Foundation. The head of the local chapter had asked Jessi where she wanted to go.

"The moon," she had replied. We settled for second best.

The physical therapy for her chest was often painful. Somehow we realized the same effect could be achieved from tossing Jessi around in a blanket . She would start laughing and bring up copious amounts of mucus. Outside regulatory agencies have visiting teams that monitor hospital quality. They may review random charts. Jessi's chart might have read "Please toss Jessi in a blanket for 10 minutes, three times a day. Do not let her fall."

My favorite Jessi story goes like this.

"Watcha got Jess?"

"My new sewing machine, Dr. Moore."

"Watcha doing?"

"I'm sewing a duck pattern around the edges of my hospital pillow cases. It does that automatically, Dr. Moore."

"You can't do that, Jess," I warned.

"Why?" She snapped back.

"There must be a hospital rule."

Jessi then move closer, scowling eyeball to eyeball, she looked into my soul.

"So what," she spat as the conversation ended.

My friend Steve relates the story of a New York subway panhandler who wore a fake leg cast. Rattling his tin cup he collected enough change to winter in Florida. We made Jessi a similar fake leg cast to use with crutches or wheelchair. A dozen false stories accompanied this prop.

"We're ready to take your chest x-ray Jessi. Jeez, what happened to your leg? How did you do that?"

If you missed Jessi at home, there was always a new message on the answering machine, with weird, unintelligible animal noises.

Jessi and I often had long talks about boys, why God allows children to have bad diseases, and whether I was so old I would die before she did.

The third floor window on the east end of the pediatric

ward was an excellent roost for spotting rainbows.

"Sometimes when I get admitted to the hospital I'm really feeling sick. But if I can see a rainbow I feel a lot better."

As Jessi turned ten, her condition was worsening. We discussed a lung transplant with a center in Carolina, but her disease had progressed to the point where the physical and emotional cost outweighed any benefit. I finally bit the bullet and with her permission, measured her blood carbon dioxide level. It was very high. If she had been a newborn, we would have placed her on a ventilator.

With everyone on board, we started to withdraw treatment. During Jessi's last hospitalization we prepared for her death. Jess asked many questions but we only had some answers for some of them. On the last day Jessi mumbled that she was "ready to let go". The nurses and I took turns at pushing the button on the morphine pump that we used for pain control. When the total dose of narcotic was tallied, it was not excessive. Jessi died quietly, surrounded by her family.

The church was full at her funeral mass. Schoolmates, family, friends, and medical personal all remembered her laughter and courage in the face of daily pain. At the end of the service we all sobbed uncontrollably. The last entry in her hospital record is a poem by Veronica Shoffstall. It ends with these prophetic words-

And you learn-
And you learn-
And with every goodbye, you learn.

Pictured: Jessi

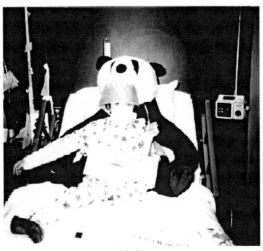

16

LET IT SNOW

I always thought it was a cliché or a chamber of commerce marketing ploy, but it turns out that in Maine we really do get a lot more snow than other parts of the country. Our annual average snowfall is seventy inches. That is less than the Snow Belt across Michigan and upstate New York, but higher than most Midwest and western states, excluding high elevations. We also beat a number of towns and cities in Alaska. Leading the way for Maine at 111 inches is Caribou, where once I encountered snowflakes in August. There is a seventy percent chance of a white Christmas in our area.

The blizzard I remember best was on the day before Christmas in 1970. The annual employee party was that afternoon at the office. My secretary and I trudged several blocks north to pick up sandwiches at the caterer. On the way, back the strength of the winter storm became evident. It quickly became difficult to walk back into the wind through the accumulating snow. At least we had food if we became stranded.

We eventually struggled to the office. Cars had become stalled on nearby Route One. Their occupants had wandered to our office, attracted to the brightly lit and gaily decorated bay window. Those stranded were pleased to find hot food and cold beverages laid out. Many were "from away", as the locals had long since headed home to avoid the drifts. The strangers even started singing with us. A few, in jest, asked about the possibility of spending the night sleeping on an exam table. The out-of-state partiers were generally amazed at our hospitality and camaraderie. Gradually our unexpected guests filtered back to their cars as our city plows, the size of mobile homes, did their usual excellent work. Farther south on Route One, my partner directed traffic around stalled autos, wearing his signature cowboy hat. Through the blizzard, everyone thought he was a state trooper.

Maine has a long tradition of downhill skiing and a number of excellent resorts. Short skis, which have once again come back into vogue, were the rage in the '70s. With these, I could carve tight turns and negotiate trails that were otherwise beyond my ability. Unfortunately, "shorties" have a tendency to become airborne, which once led to an unexpected visit to a family doctor's office in Waitsfield Vermont.

"How'd you get that head gash, Doctor Moore?"

"Actually just skied off a cliff during a whiteout on Sugarbush. Shorty skis."

"I can suture that," he offered. "You're not the first, not even the first doctor."

"I see from your diploma that you have your boards in Dermatology and Syphilis from New York."

"Yup. Not much syphilis here, so I do a little of everything. Moved to Vermont to avoid taxes," offered the family doctor.

"Did that work out?"

"Nope."

Leaving the office, I was holding a gauze pad to my newly sutured scalp when an elderly farm lady said, "You're going back up on the mountain, aren't you? You skiers are all crazy."

"Yes ma'am", I answered. "All day ticket."

Knock on wood, my only winter fender-bender occurred shortly after my arrival. I was headed northeast down a marginally plowed hill in Biddeford. The locals still tell of a past Francophone mayor whose credo was, roughly translated, "God, she brings the snow in the fall and takes it in the spring." There will be no snow left in May, regardless of removal. Why spend a lot of money?

But, there are consequences. My VW brakes failed to grip the gently sloping ice rink, while two blocks away the HUMPTY DUMPTY potato chip truck was having a similar problem trying to turn left in front of me. With a gentle, slow motion crash, I became the first pediatrician in America to injure a children's nursery icon. Our office staff refused to accept my excuse for tardiness. My nurse's cartoonist husband crafted artwork that I still cherish. The local auto body shop did put Humpty Dumpty back together again.

The call came in again during a blizzard. A week old infant was coughing, breathing rapidly and had poor color.

Both city ambulances were on other trips to the medical center.

With the choke in full, I headed my Scout east to Old

19

Orchard Beach. The snow was icy and blowing sideways. The infamous OOB rotary loomed menacingly. This maze demands the skill of a NASA pilot to survive the stoplight-free slalom course. The tangle spit me out onto the trailer park road. I had to blast through several high snow banks. This was the exact excuse for the extra expense of 4WD. Men are just boys but their toys are bigger.

It was the standard white trailer with green wreath. Mother had not underestimated the problem. The struggling infant was the color of Garside's black raspberry ice cream, a reference to a local dairy product. The phrase was used occasionally in our nursery to describe poorly oxygenated newborns. Crackles resonated throughout the infant's chest.

A small oxygen tank, left over from football season, nestled inside my bag. In retrospect, it was probably illegal to carry it in a passenger vehicle. After placing the mask over the baby's face, the blue hue lessened.

"Hey doc. I can't go to the hospital because I have no sitter. But you can put the baby in her bassinette in the passenger seat."

There were no infant car seats yet. Plan A did not appeal to me, especially if the weather worsened and we were stuck.

Plan B involved getting a sitter. The phones were working and we were soon in business. I called ahead to the emergency room. The trip to the hospital was uneventful with sparse traffic, and we all skidded into the ambulance entrance with great flourish. After several days, antibiotics and good nursing cured the infant. I initially considered a motivational sticker for my Scout cab, like the storks on an ambulance -but the idea seemed bit tacky.

The Humpty Dumpty Crash
Art work by Bob Black

HOUSE CALLS

It was a quiet morning when a Saco family watched in horror as my car entered their driveway too quickly and nearly sideswiped a cow. I sheepishly went inside and introduced myself. The sick child shivered with fever in her bedroom. Her siblings, all dressed in their Sunday best, peered anxiously around the door frame. After greeting her, I gathered my stethoscope, eased onto the quilt and splintered the pine bed frame. The bedless and wailing child was given a shot of penicillin, to add insult to injury. The family did not receive a bill. Years later, however, I received an invitation to the child's wedding.

Why did I, like many doctors, make house calls decades ago? Most mothers were at home during the day and often lacked transportation to our office. Moreover, there were no full time physicians in the emergency room. If you didn't make a call on a family during the day, you might see them at the hospital at 2 AM. Also, a handful of my patients were bedridden with a variety of chronic illnesses. These children would often have pumps and tubes arranged around their home hospital bed. Elaborate wall calendars would be covered with rainbow-colored markers indicating hourly medicine schedules and weekly blood draws. It was a stark reminder of the effort required by the parents and visiting nurses.

House calls were a peek into family life that you could never get from the office. One winter I made home visits to two very similar older apartments, only a block apart.

A single mother of three complained her dwelling was too old to clean properly. The odor was overwhelming, beyond description.

The twin rental on the next street was occupied by an unwed teen mother her young infant. It looked as if she had waxed the floors, walls, and ceilings. You could have eaten off the floor.

My black bag looked like a big loaf of bread. The top contained many little compartments with medication, syringes, diagnostic tools and a bunch of other gear. You tried to carry everything that might be needed. A doctor could appear foolishly inept if he had to retreat back to the office for missing equipment. As medical students in New York City, three of us made a house call on a young adult with rheumatoid arthritis. Unfortunately, we neglected to bring the leads for the EKG machine. I drew the short stick and had to make a forty-block round trip.

One winter, I was called to a house on the ocean at Biddeford Pool. A northeasterly blizzard was working up and nobody was coming into the office. As I headed south, the snow piled up quickly. After helping several drivers get out of snowdrifts and back on the road, it was finally my turn. Approaching the house, my car skidded up onto a snow bank, leaving all wheels flailing in the air. A group of laughing fisherman picked my small vehicle off the pile and back onto the street.

I arrived at the cottage which overlooked a menacing sea. The young child had pneumonia and received the usual injection of penicillin. Mother invited me for tea.

As is often the case, we found that we had some friends in common and engaged in small talk. Every few minutes an imposing black wave would slam against the picture window. It looked like a car wash. The small house seemed to lift off its foundation for a split second while dishes rattled in the dining room. My new friend noted my ashen countenance.

"Don't worry, doctor," she said. "This really isn't much of a storm. Now that one last March was a doozy! "

My trip home was uneventful. The office staff asked if there were any problems.

"Fairly routine", I lied.

Sometimes the hardest task was actually finding the house of the sick child in this time before global positioning and cell phones. One snowy December evening a call came in from a new trailer park. On the phone mother said I couldn't miss it. It was a generic white trailer with green wreath. When I arrived at the hilltop, dozens of similarly decorated mobile homes twinkled below. The manager's white trailer sported a green wreath.

"Can't miss it doc," he said. " First right, then next two lefts, down the hill to Pheasant Drive. Can't miss it".

His instructions seemed clear, after two loops through the park my Scout arrived back at the office trailer.

"Couldn't find Pheasant Drive."

"Actually, I haven't put the sign up yet", the manager responded in typical Maine style.

"Get into the Jeep!" came my order. "You are about to witness a real old-fashioned house call."

We arrived shortly.

"Didn't have any problems finding us Doc? White trailer with green wreath."

Children with flashlights were often placed on the porch to guide me into the proper driveway for a house call. Alternatively the porch light flicked on and off as a standard signal. As mobile phones came into use, home visit requests diminished but, now there was no excuse. Despite direct verbal communication with the expecting family, navigation problems continued.

"Hey Doc. Can you hear me? What's the matter with you? You've driven past our house seven times. Pay attention!"

House calls are now seen as being an inefficient use of time, manpower and money. Although semi-retired, I still make an occasional home visit for friends or neighbors. The encounter always strips medicine to its core - sometimes anxious parents, an ill child, and the doctor with a few medical instruments. I always feel my most important.

DRIVE WHAT YOU ARE

It was my 35th high school reunion, in the suburbs of New York City. I was trading stories with Tony who was now living in California. Suddenly Tony blurted, "Do you know in California, you are what you drive?"

"Tony," I responded. "In Maine you drive what you are!"

I was stating the obvious. If you were a fisherman you would drive a truck. If a doctor you sported a 4WD, which actually used to set us apart before the sport utility craze towards the end of the millennium. Besides, the parents in my practice didn't want me driving a high end car. Occasionally they would spot such as car in my parking lot - usually belonging to summer visitor.

"Nice car, doc. Where'd you get that?"

My first car after marriage was a Volkswagen Beetle. It was easy to maintain and served me well in the mild climate of Washington, D.C. That was not the case in Maine. It tended to hang up on snow banks with four wheels spinning in the air. The engine was air-cooled, as was the heating system, which led to some interesting commutes when the temperature dipped below zero.

My father-in-law, who was well known in the Navy for his practical jokes, poured a Costco-sized bag of confetti into the back of the car as Wendy and I left our wedding reception. Years later, it seemed that every time I made a house call, clouds of shredded paper would rise from the car.

27

I always feared the waiting parents, watching from the window, would question the age and maturity of the confetti-covered new doctor ringing the doorbell.

My first dream car was an International Harvester Scout, aptly named as it really did sound like a harvester. My children claimed temporary hearing loss on long rides in this prehistoric SUV. On house calls, my families could hear me blocks away. This beast shared the same major flaw with other four-wheel drive vehicles of this era – exterior locking hubs. One had to venture into blizzard conditions, touch bare fingers to painfully cold metal hubs and attempt to twist them in below zero weather - sort of like buttoning your shirt while wearing boxing gloves.

I next purchased a Jeep CJ5 when Wendy was out of town. Today, I would never make a major family purchase in this manner. When first married I wrote the checks, made all the decisions, and was brought morning coffee in bed. At some time over the next forty years the roles reversed, and this has surely been for the better.

My children said it was my first cool car. It was very cool. In fact, my family voted it the coldest car in North America. Despite supplemental heating, I often worried about arriving at the emergency room in a hypothermically incoherent state. It also had exterior locking external hubs. Just at this time the hospital hired full-time emergency room doctors which made need for 4WD less imperative.

The Jeep inevitably began to rust out. My mechanically

talented first son began to pop-rivet aluminum sheets to the underbody. He felt that any problems with the frame could be addressed with pop-rivets and duct tape. We prayed that there were no occult frame defects because the family budget did not allow the purchase of home welding equipment. My son drooled at the very thought. One Saturday morning I spent several hours doing surgery on rusted electrical wiring in the tailgate.

I finally sold the jeep to Dan the Auto Body Man, a former patient and now a parent in my practice. For years afterward, as the morning mist parted for a split second on Route One, I could occasionally see Dan driving my Jeep in the oncoming lane with a grim look on his face. He says he would often take my name in vain, when a puddle would short out the rear electrical system. He did, however, offer to paint the Canadian flag on the top of Wendy's red Escort.

My last muscle car was a Nissan van with sliding doors. It had the silhouette of a toaster. My children refused to ride in it or drive it. They called it the Coke Machine. It had good winter visibility because it was fifteen feet in the air. You could always find it in the mall parking lot. It would hold three rooms worth of college dorm room furniture. But, it was aerodynamically unstable in moderate wind and underpowered. You couldn't run cruise control and AC simultaneously. On its last run, I had to drive it back from Boston without a clutch. After slowly cruising through several tollbooths while tossing coins through the night air and then rolling past several neighborhood stop signs, I arrived home ashen and mute.

My children smiled smugly.

My cars since then have been fairly vanilla. All I needed was a battery that would stay alive in the dead of winter, quality temperature modulation in both directions, and as Wendy says, cool tunes. I always prided myself in having the oldest car in the doctor's parking lot and, when I performed on-site sports physicals, in the high school student parking lot. It was a badge of honor.

The teen daughter of a doctor gave the ultimate compliment to me. They were both walking in from the hospital parking lot one Sunday morning. I was just getting out of my car.

" That's Dr. Moore", he informed.

"Daddy. He can't be a doctor. Look at the car he's driving."

HOW DO?

Prior to the advent of mobile telephones, it was sometimes difficult to physically locate a doctor. This did not instill confidence in patients. I remember the story of a wealthy matron who signed out of a New England resort hospital and commandeered an ambulance to New York Hospital after hearing "If there are any doctors in the hospital, please go to the emergency room" over the loudspeakers. Recently the nurses in small hospital in Texas called 911 when a post operative patient experienced difficulty.

In our Air Force hospital there was a silent ten number paging system with green displays in every corridor. My Navy pilot cousin once told me that if his colleagues forgot their code word for the day and had to be escorted out of unauthorized air space, their promotions would end. I would have been demoted to airman first class if that had been the Air Force rule. In an emergency the paging lights would flash red. The nuclear attack DRILL blazed 0 through 8 and Armageddon was 0 through 9. Of course I could never remember which was which.

When I first moved to Maine communications were simple but effective. Mr. L ran the answering system. His office even had an old telephone switchboard with tips and plugs just like the old movies.

Mr. L always answered with a brisk but pleasant "How do?" If you were not at home, he always knew where you were hiding. In addition, he would offer unsolicited but useful comments about the family on the other end of the line. My very first phone call from Mr. L went something like this –

"How do, Dr. Moore? Welcome to Maine. Mrs. A just called. Her daughter is dying of an asthma attack, but she always says that."

According to urban legend, Mr. L once suggested to a mother in early labor that she try the local veterinarian because all of the obstetricians were out of town.

Because there were neither pagers nor cell phones, you would have to tell people where you were going. It was common practice to arrive for a house call and have the mother ask you to call the hospital to discuss a different case. On other occasions I would come home to find Wendy on the back porch flicking the light on and off, rotating an arm overhead with her index finger extended, like a baseball umpire signaling a home run. This was our secret code indicating that I was needed back at the hospital.

Phone calls in the middle of the night are part of being a doctor. I would ritually flip a couple of switches and route the office line into my home from 11 PM to 7 AM, giving me two live phones on my bedside table – one private and one medical. The reason I answered my own office phone late at night was because in an emergency, parents or operators often forwarded erroneous phone numbers. I worried that I would either fail to locate a sick child or wake up an innocent household.

Bizarre questions become even more so in the middle of the night. I'm talking about 3 AM. Here are some of my favorites -

- My child is wheezing and our dog just ate the inhaler.
- I'm here at college and I couldn't sleep, so I thought I would call you.
- I was calling for a Tylenol dose. I didn't realize you were in the office. Could you schedule a sports physical for my child?
- We've just had a contraceptive failure and I can't find a gynecologist in the yellow pages who doesn't sound Catholic.
- How often do you give the Twelve-Hour Nasal Spray?

Often the man of the household was not the best person to describe his child's illness. We now understand that women will, on the average, run through eighty thousand words a day and that men will issue forth with a quarter of that number. By suppertime Dad may have run through his quota. It would go like this -

"Hi. This is Dr. Moore returning your call."

"Oh, Hi Dr. Moore. Mr. Smith here. Yes here's what the problem is. Well John or is it Suzy had had this. Ah. Tylenol. Maybe rash. Possibly several days. Hmmm. Let me get the wife."

or sometimes even –

33

"Hi. This is Dr. Moore returning your call."

"Who?"

"Dr. Moore. Is your wife there?"

"Why do you want her?"

"She called."

"We didn't call you."

"You did," I insisted.

"Nobody sick here", and finally, from the background, "For bleep sake Harry, Sean has had a fever of 104 for five days. Gimme the phone."

In the good old days, a triple-decker would have one phone for the whole apartment building on the first floor. The message was relayed to the top floor like the childhood game of *Pass It On.*

"Hi. Can I talk to Mrs. Cote? This is Dr. Moore. She has a sick child."

"Hey Doris, Go upstairs and tell Charlene that Dr. Moore is on the phone."

"I can't go up more than one floor because of my knee."

Two minute pause.

"Hi Joan. Can you tell Charlene upstairs that some doctor is on the phone?"

Longer pause. "Hi Charlene, the phone is for you. Something about a coat."

"It's probably about the layaway plan for my new coat. Tell them I'll be in next week for a payment."

The process is reversed and finally I get the message.

"Charlene says she'll be in next week to pay you."

Finally, a family from a town deep in the woods came to Saco to spend time at a local amusement park. Their child became ill with meningitis and was admitted to our hospital. Luckily, the infection was not highly contagious. After a few days, our now smiling vacationer was ready to travel back north by ambulance to finish her intravenous treatment. We called the family's local hospital numerous times in the middle of a weekday, but were unable to get anyone on the phone. I am all for quietude and rural rhythms, but none of us could understand this lapse.

THE EYES HAVE IT

Recently, some high priests of medicine have speculated that technology will render irrelevant the art of physical diagnosis. Their somewhat dystopic vision is one where the patient would fill out a questionnaire, have a total body scan via the nurse or doctor's cell phone, and a receive a blood evaluation through intact skin. Several days later, they could call a toll free number to obtain a possible diagnosis by entering in his credit card number. This whole process might not even involve words or conversation.

I would at least partially disagree with this premise. I rapidly recall a number of children when the diagnostic use of sight, sound, smells, and touch helped uncover a difficult diagnosis. A mixture of both technology and physical diagnosis is often more helpful than either alone. Interaction with the child, often on mother's lap, gives a sense that the doctor thorough and caring.

As medical students we all revered the art of physical diagnosis. As paid night lab tech I would often swap rapid test results for a peek at an intern's sick patient. Later in our training, we hung around the city hospital ER like gym rats. The interns and residents were usually cooperative in showing us instructive cases.

The New York Dermatology Society would host quarterly seminars featuring unusual, often tropical diseases. Paid rashy patients sat in cubicles with signage announcing their particular malady. I assumed they were not contagious and known to the health department.

The scene looked like a county fair. For the medical students it was a free night out.

In training, we would often wander down into the hospital basement to watch several simultaneous autopsies. There often was the awed surprise of a missed diagnosis in this pre scan era. During my pediatric residency I opted for a pathology elective where I performed autopsies and signed out tissue diagnoses. In past years an office microscope would help make an early diagnosis of meningitis or kidney infection. This tool is now being removed from some medical school training.

I was summoned to the emergency room one humid summer day. A twelve-year-old boy had been found unconscious in the road near his parent's ocean side cottage. His parents had been out shopping. The boy was comatose but breathing on his own. The parents had arrived and were appropriately frantic. The lab tests, including spinal fluid evaluation were all unremarkable.

A quick exam yielded no evidence of trauma. But I detected a slight fruity odor to his breath. Not the usual acetone nail polish remover smell of diabetic acidosis, but more of a pineapple fragrance.

"Can we have the lab do an alcohol level?" I asked.

"Doc, there's no history of abuse and the parents are straight shooters. We're just wasting money," emergency room physician protested.

I repeated my request to the nurse. The alcohol level was three times the legal limit. We were able to treat the child accordingly.

When our ill child recovered, he sheepishly confessed to sampling the flavored 100 proof rum sitting on the living room table. His chums had a few sips of beer from the fridge but vanished down the beach when his friend began to stagger. There is no lab test for nasal rum odor.

"Hey Dr. Moore, the kid with croup has green eyes," offered Dr. B.

That sounded like a strange comment. Dr. B was spending a month with me. He was a local friend who was a third year pediatric resident in a western state. He was very bright and later rated as a top pediatrician in his area.

The child's mother had called at midnight. Her son had been seen for croup by his pediatrician earlier. The croup had worsened. I prescribed the usual "head-in-the-freezer" home treatment and asked them to come to my office in the morning. It was his regular doctor's day off.

"Actually some kids with green eyes do get croup", I quipped.

"No. I'm talking about the whites of his eyes. Sometimes patients with myelogenous leukemia with very high white blood cell counts develop a green tinge to their sclera. I think the leukemia pressing on his trachea is

39

causing the croup."

I visually confirmed Dr. B's findings, though the pea-soup hue was very subtle. A quick blood smear and chest x-ray validated the leukemia diagnosis -steroids and radiation therapy quickly quieted his airway problem.

One wintry Sunday afternoon I was in the office, aware of an impending ice storm. A grandmother called to say that her nine month-old grandson had a high fever but otherwise seemed well. I directed her to bring the child up to the office as soon as possible so we could all get back home promptly.

On arrival, the baby was alert, investigating my medical equipment, with only a moderate fever. His exam was unrevealing. Or was it?

I turned up the lights and removed his diaper and T-shirt. After a few moments I noted two tiny red dots over his lower abdomen. The dots did not disappear when I stretched the skin, indicating a true hemorrhage. A small percentage of children with fever and hemorrhagic skin dots will have a blood stream infection. It used to be one in twenty. With modern immunizations it is now one in two hundred.

Wendy expertly held the now-frightened baby while I drew a blood culture and started antibiotics. We all then skated over to the adjacent hospital emergency room. By the time the child was triaged he had several dozen of these dots. The next morning his blood culture grew out meningococcus bacteria. Though the disease carries a ten per cent mortality rate, the baby recovered. His white blood count was normal, not unusual early in the illness. There is no specific blood test for little red dots.

Soon after I arrived in Maine, I was asked to consult on an older teen. He had been admitted to the hospital with weight loss and fatigue. Blood tests, chest x-ray and exam by his private physician were normal. Several years prior a melanoma had been excised from his back. The margins had been all free of tumor.

The adolescent seemed to appear healthy and in good spirits. We joked and talked about sports. My examination was unremarkable. I was still puzzled and without a diagnosis. I went back and redid the exam. High in the left armpit I just barely managed to feel a tiny gritty area with the tip of my index finger.

I asked the surgeon to biopsy the lymph node I felt. The report revealed malignant metastatic melanoma.

Another time I was beckoned to the emergency room at 5 AM. A three-month-old premature twin was seizing. Mother explained that her baby had been acting well until she found him convulsing in his crib. We quickly stabilized the child with intravenous phenobarbital. There were no signs of trauma. CT and MRI had not yet been invented. The skull x-ray was normal.

A second examination of the right retina revealed a tiny area of hemorrhage - evidence of shaken baby syndrome. This was the only marker for child abuse. No blood test would have made this diagnosis. Appropriate medical, social, and legal measures were taken.

"Dr. Moore. I've written all my symptoms on this yellow legal pad. It takes up three sides."

Of course, it was 4:30 PM on a Friday preceding my weekend off. My last scheduled patient was a somewhat overweight teenage girl. I scanned her neat cursive writing. "Poor sleep. Can't play basketball. Fatigue. Weak muscles. Decreasing school grades. Irregular periods. Weight loss." I would be talking to this teen for at least an hour.

Then I noticed a strange phenomenon. Her body appeared to be ever so slightly lifting off the table in time to her pulse.

I wish that all diagnoses were this straightforward. The several dozen symptoms that she had written down matched the textbook description hyperthyroidism, and lab tests confirmed this. The diagnosis would have been made eventually, but we might have spent big dollars on other testing. Moreover, serious problems such as cardiac irregularities can arise from untreated hyperthyroidism. After treatment, all of her symptoms disappeared. There is no blood test for bouncing.

Another time I was called by a family practitioner in an adjacent city. A week old baby was ashen and unresponsive from vomiting. The only abnormality was undescended testicles, noted in the nursery. I asked that the baby boy be sent to our emergency room, stat.

On arrival, the infant appeared to be critically ill. As I

asked the nurse to remove the diaper, I predicted abnormal looking genitalia. There is a condition where the fetal adrenal glands produce male hormones instead

of cortisone. In females, parts of the genitalia are stimulated and the extra tissue looks like a small penis. This baby girl looked like a boy without testicles.

My guess was correct. Without cortisone, the infant had a dangerously low sodium level and was minutes away from dying. With intravenous fluids, cortisone, and later reconstructive surgery, our patient would lead a normal life a as girl – though any future babies would have to be delivered via Cesarean section to protect the repaired genitalia. A blood sodium test exists, but an abnormal value doesn't come with an asterisk telling you why.

I am certain that any physician could recall similar stories. Even with new technology I still view medicine as an art rather than a science.

SUMMER PEOPLE

Our summer visitors are often lovely people. My wife would comment, "of course, many are Canadians." There are only a few downsides. Your supermarket may be unrecognizable from Memorial Day to Labor Day. Traffic may be a problem. Lodging for your visitors can be hard to find.

One evening during the Independence Day crush, I encountered two young male Quebecois in my parking lot. In typically excellent English, they asked me if I would rent them a room for the weekend. They told me they had scoured the area for the entire afternoon and that there were no beds available anywhere. Initially I thought they had mistaken our modern, comfortable office for a motel, but it became apparent that they knew exactly where they were; when they indicated that their sleeping bags would fit just so on our plush examining tables. I am a seasoned hitchhiker and backpacker who has been helped in a pinch by strangers more times than I can remember, so I seriously considered this request. Imagining a host of possible scenarios on Monday morning snapped me back to reality. Bon voyage.

That same summer, a red Porsche accelerated down the hill in front of my house. The driver had to be "from away", as locals knew the road ended right past my house, twenty feet above the Saco River. I listened carefully but heard no splash after the squealing of brakes. The car retreated back in reverse into my drive.

"Do you know of any free camping spots? All the camp grounds want money," the young French Canadian complained.

The lush green lawn of the doctor next door beckoned. We had conducted a decade-long practical joke war. He had recently magic markered R and L on the tops of my new green canvas operating room shoes. It was time for revenge. I leaned across his string bikini clad partner in the passenger seat and started to point. Then, remembering my neighbor's shotgun collection, I gestured back up the road, and offered some low-cost suggestions.

"You need a new hospital, Dr. Moore. The paint is falling off the ceiling."

"I know, Mrs. B. It's in the planning stage. How's the care?"

"It's excellent. You and the nurses are always available for us."

This family was vacationing from Riviere du Loup Quebec, on the mouth of the St. Lawrence River. Marie was age three or four when she arrived in our emergency room with a perforated appendix and a belly full of pus. There were no pediatric surgeons at the medical center at that time, and we depended on the general surgeons at our local hospital to step up and perform excellent lifesaving surgery on sick children.

Dr. Ray did an emergency appendectomy and washed the infected fluid out of her abdomen. I landed the task of managing her postoperative fluids and medicine. We did not have the best antibiotics at that time, and we had to give Marie all of her calories intravenously. We did not know whether she would survive the first week.

Fortunately, after three weeks Marie was ready to head north. The French-speaking nurses and clergy had comforted the family far better than my efforts. Everyone hugged and kissed at discharge. The father discretely asked about payment. Dr. Ray and I asked him to just send the insurance forms down when he reached home. I knew from prior experiences that the Provincial Health Plan would pay us something.

"I want to pay both of you now in cash," insisted the grateful father in perfect English. "I will send the forms later."

He pulled a gigantic roll of American fifties from his pocket and made Dr. Ray and I tally up our fees in public, in front of several nurses. It didn't look good, but he would not relent and we accepted the payment. We heard later that Marie was healthy and present at the first day of school.

One summer we admitted a toddler from Montreal who had a high fever. The mother was an attractive television producer. We found common ground when it turned out that my favorite Quebecois movie, *La Guerre des Tuques,* was produced and directed by a good friend of hers. We became such good pals so quickly that she suddenly asked me if she could watch the spinal tap I was about to perform on her child. Luckily, the procedure went smoothly.

47

As my senior partner had done, after a few years I developed a clientele of families who were only here during the summer. Many were from the Cincinnati area, referred by their local pediatricians who knew me from my training days. Some were from the New York suburbs, and we had friends in common. Sometimes the young visitors were booby-trapped, with seemingly minor complaints hiding much more serious diagnosis.

A family vacationing from Little Rock brought their five-year-old child, Christopher, to the office. He was complaining about pain in his left upper arm, but he also had a fever. X-rays revealed an infection at of the top of the humerus. Thirty five years later I reconnected with his parents at church. They have moved back to the family home in Ocean Park.

Mrs. B recalls, "Dr. Moore, you offered to send us to Boston, but we trusted you to treat Christopher here".

So, I admitted Christopher to our local hospital and treated him with intravenous clindamycin. This new antibiotic was attracted to bone like a coon cat to sardines. It was also effective when given orally – a huge benefit for later home therapy.

Through his mother, I recently contacted Christopher in Denver where he is now a teacher - enjoying skiing and mountain biking. He writes: " I fell down the stairs, if my memory is correct, and chipped the bone in my shoulder and that is what started the infection. I remember the nurses and my parents telling me that I had a "bug" in my arm. At that age, all I could think of was a black insect with antennae and legs crawling

48

around my arm. What an imagination!"

The fever disappeared in several days. We were winning. The bone infection was probably a staphylococcus, but not the super-resistant variety we see today. With the help of Upjohn Pharmaceuticals, I was able to prove that Christopher could sustain high antibiotic levels when given clindamycin by mouth. That earned him a trip back to Arkansas where he made a good recovery.

Another summer visitor arrived from Massachusetts with a wound between his first two toes that was leaking pus. He had sustained a laceration in this area several weeks before. As far as I could tell, it had been sutured promptly.

Tourists flock to my neighborhood so they can sit on the beach, and sand has a nasty way of migrating into foot lacerations. I learned this the hard way. During my first summer in Maine, I was faced with several of my sutured foot lacerations, which had become infected. One of my nurses solved the mystery when she found out that most of these kids had been frolicking on the beach. I remembered this when I saw these complications. His mother just wanted an antibiotic refill, but after some back and forth, she agreed to an x-ray. Unfortunately, the films showed a bone infection that had destroyed part of a metatarsal bone. The family lived in suburban Boston so I was able to refer them Boston Children's Hospital, surely one of the best in the world.

A few summers back, I was lumbering down Ferry

49

Beach, dragging two garbage bags stuffed full of seaweed. A summer lady approached, wearing a stylish flowered top, numerous silver bracelets, and a beautiful straw hat. I was dressed in old ripped blue jeans, a t-shirt from the football team that I care for, and a baseball hat advertising the local barbecue joint.

"Hello there. What do you have in the bags?"

"Seaweed," I said. The smell from the bags was overpowering.

"Why do you do that?" The lady questioned.

"Garden," I grunted.

"Does it work?"

I was tempted to respond with " I lied to you about the garden. I just like to lug heavy smelly bags around the beach. It's really fun." But I am not really prone to sarcasm.

"Yes it does seem to work. Have a nice summer."

Mainers have a reputation for provincialism, but I find that summer vacationers are almost always courteous and friendly guests. No one can deny that they are vital to our economy. Come back and see us next summer, but leave your child's illness at home.

DAVID

David arrived at our community hospital in August 1972. His parents were visiting relatives in Ocean Park. Father was a fledgling banker in Montreal. The cold Atlantic ocean water may have induced labor.

David weighed just over two pounds. He was ten to twelve weeks early by dates but looked a bit older. There were no newborn intensive care units in Maine. David's parents did not wish to transfer him to Boston. Our Air National Guard could not fly him out of the country. A six or eight hour ambulance trip to Montreal would have been fatal.

"Doctor Moore, do the best you can. If he survives fine, if not we understand."

Can you imagine a parent saying that in 2010? The parents may have figured that if Dr. Moore had the good judgment to marry a Canadian, he would have similar skills in caring for their newborn.

He was a fighter and needed an intravenous for less than a day. Jaundice was treated with fluorescent lights. His immature lungs improved rapidly and he was weaned off oxygen after several days. By day three, his weight was 1 lb 13 oz. Formula feedings were given by tube.

His major problem was apnea, or "forgetting to breathe". Each morning the nurses would give us a running account of these spells. Often they had to hand ventilate our northern visitor. This is called "bagging"

51

but not like in the supermarket. The manual ventilators are teeny versions of those you see in the TV Emergency Room shows. We had no mechanical ventilators in 1972. A short time later, we did discover some unused state money and purchased a Bird Mark 7 ventilator. At the time, I compared this machine to the Edsel Ford. Those of you receiving Social Security will remember this failed auto. But, we may have been the first hospital in the state to get a newborn on and successfully off a mechanical ventilator.

David tolerated his tube feedings and slowly gained weight. His apnea episodes resolved. This progress was a tribute to our nursing staff. Without their skilled care, David would not have survived. They rocked, comforted, fed and sang to our tiny summer vacationer. Visitors were restricted to parents and relatives. His survival was not strictly a medical miracle, but it required skill and dedication from all his caregivers.

David went home to Montreal well under the usual discharge weight of five pounds. With kisses and hugs the family headed north on Route 5. We learned that Mum and Dad had no problem bringing a new citizen back across the border.

That's not the end of the story. In the large urban hospitals, newborn specialists often lose follow-up on their premature infants. David and his family often spent summer vacations with their aunt in Ocean Park. We would have tearful reunions in the waiting room. At age four David was playing hard and speaking well. The only residual problem was a slight hearing loss.

I would say hi to David about every five years when he visited relatives in Maine. He had the usual dry Canadian humor. In his twenties David was living in an apartment in Toronto. I envisioned he was working with computers. His cousin sent me a recent update while I was out of town. Much to my surprise the new photo shows a solidly- built smiling long haul trucker who lives in Texas. He may not have been able to get his 18-wheeler in our parking lot.

Addendum – at the time of my book's final edit David has sent me a picture of him and his new bride, taken at a Las Vegas chapel last year. You will find it in the photo album in the back of the book.

Pictured: David and Dr. Moore

HAITI

"Why not come down with us to Haiti for 10 days in January to open the clinic, Dr. Moore?" Asked nurse Jean.

"Let me think about it for a day", I flipped back, as if I had been asked to a neighborhood barbecue.

It was 1986 and I had just experienced a chance encounter with Jimmy, Laura and nurse Jean. We were all collecting gratis orthopedic equipment from a retiring colleague. Earlier in the year this Baptist group had constructed a medical clinic in northern Haiti. They would return in a few months with supplies to open the center. Due to a scheduling conflict, I had to decline a similar invitation twenty years earlier during my training - this time a three month stint at the Albert Schweitzer Clinic in central Haiti. I had always regretted missing the adventure.

Now, I felt obligated to put up or shut up. With support from Wendy and some unspent Christmas money, I agreed.

The four of us flew down to Haiti aboard a Mission Aviation Fellowship vintage DC9, flown by retired Eastern Airline pilots and their "stewardess" wives. Some of these aviators had probably guided these same aircraft over Burma during World War II. Laughing dentists from Ohio also joined us in the cargo netting and portable jump seats. When we refueled in St. George, I imagined I saw Humphrey Bogart sitting next to the piano in the thatched airport lounge.

In several previous trips, this Maine church had helped to build a medical clinic in Terrier Rouge, a town of about 20,000 in the north of Haiti. It is part of a community services complex that also includes an elementary school, a large orphanage, and a church. The clinic has a lab, pharmacy, waiting room, and exam area. The whole complex is guided by the firm, but kind, hand of Pastor Noel. When I met him he was in his mid-50s; vigorous, humorous, and very hard-working. He is the spiritual and economic leader of the area, in an ecumenical sense. His Russian Lada car was instantly recognized by district children who greeted him with whoops of "Hey Pastor". The reverend was continually doling out food, money, and spiritual advice to all, regardless of religious persuasion.

As with most third world countries, visiting Haiti is an emotional roller coaster. The eye flips from stark poverty to the awe-inspiring beauty of the Sans Souci Palace or Citadelle. On the same day you can hear the terror of political riots and the sounds of a smartly dressed fifteen member choir, singing in perfect five part harmony. Haiti leads the Western hemisphere in poverty, population density, and birth rate. Two hundred years ago it was the gem of the Caribbean with the highest literacy rate in the western hemisphere. In 1987 the average Haitian, if employed, made one hundred thirty dollars per year. Though food was relatively inexpensive at that time, baby formula was still thirty cents per bottle.

The language is Creole, basically phonetic French with local flair. Skin becomes po, water dlo, and ear zorey. "Tap-taps" are the gaily-painted minivans with home town destinations painted on the front and religious, political, and commercial messages, such as Jesus Saves and Air France, emblazoned the sides. These moving billboards are always filled with passengers, and on the roof are more passengers, bags of cement, charcoal, hens, and goats. Sixty cents will get you one mile or sixty.

Pepsi has signs all over the country with the double entendre of the "new generation". In the preceding year, the Baptist group had to cut their visit short as the January Revolution exploded and Baby Doc Duvalier fled to Europe. The Pastor thought it prudent to quickly hustle his American friends off the island. Fleeing southward, Reverend Noel and the Yanks bribed their way through twenty roadblocks-grabbing the last three American Airline seats out of Port au Prince.

Houses are made of sticks, dried mud, or concrete blocks, with thatched roofs and cement or dirt floors. Most have two outbuildings - a charcoal-burning kitchen and a latrine. The French engineers taught the natives that a fifty foot deep latrine would last a lifetime but forgot about the thirty foot water table in the equation. To avoid "Baby Doc's revenge" we all drank Kola or fruit juice. "Culligan" is the generic term for all bottled water - wishful thinking. It was also rumored that when the Kola factory filter was malfunctioning, well water was used . I have first hand testimony to that possible scenario.

The pastor's home was comfortable and clean. Meals were excellent and consisted of beef, goat, fish and turkey. Plantain, bananas, tomatoes, sweet potatoes and fresh fruits were served on the side. We ate small portions in this third world country, since we knew excess food would not go uneaten. When rain was abundant, local UNESCO sponsored wells provided clean water. It was also rumored that upon the arrival of any Americans, a drought would cease. Yes indeed, the torrent came on our fifth day. Haitian children generally do not enjoy the rain and they stared in wonder as Jimmy and I soaped up in bathing suits and took impromptu outdoor showers. The youngsters also marveled at the hair on my forearms.

Medical care fluctuates between barely accessible and nonexistent. The local Roman Catholic church has a clinic with a doctor who visits three hours a week. The hospital is twenty miles to the west in Cap Haitien. At times, supplies are so short that surgeons will meet the Mission Aviation Fellowship planes at the airport in the middle of an operation to obtain what is needed. Relatives must supply food for hospitalized family members.

We treated four hundred patients in five days. Patients waited for up to seven hours. In a town without watches, clocks, scales, and thermometers, accurate histories were difficult to obtain. One of the first patients was a wheezing middle aged woman. During my internship, when treating older adults, it was often difficult to tell bubbly asthma from the junky chest of heart failure. But then my switch to pediatrics solved that problem - cardiac congestion is rare in children. Now, twenty years later, the same conundrum surfaced. But the native looked sturdy and coronary heart disease would be fairly rare in a non-smoking field worker who was eating a mainly vegetarian diet. With some trepidation, I treated this woman with several teaspoons of liquid asthma medicine that had been donated by one of our drug representatives. I asked her to sit under a nearby tree for a while.

In a half an hour, my patient wandered back into the clinic with some excited friends. When I listened to her lungs again they were clear. When news of this cure spread, we received a flood of patients with cerebral palsy, strokes, and other such maladies who were unfortunately expecting similar miracles.

We ran out of some of our drug supplies from home. When Jimmy and Laura attempted to purchase more from a pharmacy in Cap Haitien we discovered prices of twenty dollars for a bottle of 100 aspirin and five dollars for a four ounce bottle of Maalox. I never did discover the reason for these prices - probably supply and demand.

We saw tuberculosis, measles, pneumonia, otitis, impetigo, worms, hysteria, anemia, trachoma with corneal scarring, dyspepsia, and a great deal of malignant hypertension. In a population that had never been exposed to antibiotics, infections cleared rapidly using half the usual dose. A baby with a huge leg abscess was cured in four days after a simple drainage. Pneumonia disappeared in two or three days. Several volunteers translated for us, but we were left on our own on the last day as they all left to watch Pastor Noel arm wrestle a newly arrived rototiller- a gift from a northern Maine congregation.

It would require dozens of pages to chronicle the warmth and gratitude of the Haitian people. A special church service was held on the evening of our arrival, complete with a large banner featuring our names. At a similar service marking our departure, Marie the clinic director said that the congregation had nothing to give us but their prayers and thanks. I stood in a circle holding hands with an elderly Haitian woman on each side. Tears were streaming down my face as we sang hymns. On the way out, many villagers shook my hand. On our last morning the children of the orphanage sang to us and gave us bon voyage speeches.

After the trip, our local hospital medical staff provided additional funding and medicine for the clinic. Over the years, we have kept some contact with the Haitians, especially when they have visited Maine. There are two children in my Maine practice with Haitian parents, so there is often updated news from Terrier Rouge. From my involvement in this project, I have learned to be very humble about the abundance we have in Maine and America. The Haitians are a special and caring people who have suffered greatly under oppressive political regimes. We can only hope and pray that with the help of the global community, conditions will improve.

BIRDS OF A FEATHER

It was 4:30 on a Saturday afternoon and I had just slipped home to feed the cat and make some coffee. I had been awake most of the previous evening, worrying about this and that. Wendy and the children were out of town. I finished my coffee and the phone rang. It was Debbie calling to say that Michael's feeding tube had come out and she could not replace it. She sounded upset. I said that I would fix it on my way back to the hospital.

Michael was three and had a progressive neurological disease that is uniformly fatal. Debbie was only seventeen when she delivered Michael, but had matured greatly since then. She knew a lot more about life and death than I did when I was her age. Debbie cared for Michael at home for his first two years, but when he could no longer take feedings by mouth and his weight had slipped to thirteen pounds Debbie came to me in tears and pleaded, "Dr. Moore, I just can't watch him starve to death." I placed Michael in a skilled-care nursing facility where he began to receive food through a tube in his throat. Unfortunately, after a few months the nursing home closed and Michael had to be transferred to an adjacent town. This proved to be a hardship for all.

Debbie was a better mother when nurses and administrators were not involved in her son's care. She tearfully asked me if she could care for her son at home, and I said yes without hesitation. She quickly mastered the art of suctioning Michael's mouth and changing his feeding tube. Since her apartment was between my

61

home and the hospital, it was not a burden to make house calls. Michael quickly gained ten pounds at home with his mother.

The pungent smell of low tide hung in the air as I drove past rows of old wooden houses on my way to replace Michael's feeding tube. Two teens embraced on the corner as I guided my Jeep into the driveway. I winked. They smiled. A grimy-faced toddler sat in the doorway with his arm around a dog. I climbed the stairs into Michael's bedroom.

Debbie said that he was quieter now. With a few twists I replaced the tube. Michael was sleeping. I wrote Debbie a few more prescriptions and walked down the narrow stairs with Michael's grandfather. I asked him to show me his pigeon loft.

We walked to the corner of the backyard and he apologized that the coop needed a cleaning. The birds went quiet as we entered. They had been fed an hour ago and were content. Grandfather snatched a bird out of mid-air and brought it down for me to see. The embossed aluminum band on its leg read "68".

"Wow, that bird is thirteen years old", I remarked.

"She sure as heck is," he replied. " Can still race good. She's got over ninety thousand miles on her. Sometimes at this age they'll be good as gold and then suddenly they'll just drop. Heart gives out."

"Ninety thousand miles . . . that's way more than my Jeep has."

"I think she's as strong as ever. But sometimes their hearts just give out", he repeated.

In the past he had told me that the pigeons easily return from points as far away as Cleveland. How they get home is a subject of intense and controversial research. There may be a magnetically sensitive area in their heads. If the homing system malfunctions, the birds will overfly their loft and eventually succumb to muscle failure.

"Maybe I've got a few more miles left," I mumbled. Suddenly, I didn't feel nearly as tired as I had an hour before.

Michael died a few months later. Debbie and I kept in touch and I cared for her son Jonathan. He now raises pigeons.

Pictured: Jonathan at a 2009 Pigeon Show
Photo by Rolla Wells

HOSPITAL TALES

Our old community hospital was a tight little organization. It lacked manpower and specialists, but the group addressed these problems with cooperation and flexibility. With a year of internal medicine training under my belt, I sometimes responded in an adult emergency. Once, unable to leave the nursery, I got on the phone and talked an internist and a nurse through the successful treatment of a seizing child with meningitis. Lab and x-ray results could generally be obtained faster than during my training, especially if the tech was a mother in my practice.

As the new kid, I was unanimously elected medical staff secretary. I would scribble minutes of meetings onto scrap paper and type them onto a half page report at home. Today, the same documentation arrives as a twenty page electronically generated report accompanied by a full DVD of the meeting.

Decades ago, for reasons I still don't understand, every hospital death was critiqued at a monthly meeting of the medical staff. In retrospect, this exercise was bizarre. Surgeons would comment on preemie care. Pediatricians would likewise offer inappropriate advice on surgical infection rates. During one memorable and heated exchange, a doctor proclaimed that he wouldn't let a colleague treat his cat.

During my early training, I sometimes encountered weird hospital rules. As an intern, my city hospital had a policy that if you arrived by ambulance, you had to be admitted. The interns and residents suspected that the regulation had been implemented to allow severely alcoholic politicians and other city workers to rest up and dry out for a few days during the winter. Only they knew the secret ambulance phone number.

This unusual situation created a huge amount of extra work for the hospital staff, and they pushed back. Finally, after weeks of negotiations with the administration, the rule was modified. If a patient delivered by ambulance was cleared by a specialist, they could go back home. Soon afterwards, a ninety-year-old woman arrived from a nursing home with mild chest pain. She received a full evaluation, and her EKG and cardiac enzymes were spot-on normal. The cardiologist pronounced her "good to go". Go she did, and she died of a massive coronary in the ambulance on the way back home. The next day the administration rescinded our hard-fought victory.

In that same emergency room, we kept a fishbowl full of subway tokens. They were given to selected patients on their way out of the drying-out room to help them make it home safely. Alas, when we interns went to our favorite pub, located just across the street to unwind after the night shift, we often found these patients bartering their transit tokens for a glass of beer. "Hey, Doc. Good to see you again. Can I buy you one for the road?"

Another rule at our local hospital stated that if a child was in the hospital for less than three days, there was no need to dictate a discharge summary. That led to some unusually convenient release times. Once, I admitted a day-old baby with seizures caused by low

66

calcium levels. The infant responded to treatment. Later, Miss L, an older woman and a gem of a record librarian, gently prodded me to produce a discharge summary. I told her that it was not needed. We conducted a polite back and forth for several days. Finally, I complied with a two sentence, tongue-in-cheek discharge summary. The crisply typed dictation was quickly returned for my signature. Luckily, it appears to have avoided review by the dreaded inspectors from the national Joint Committee, better known as JACO Jayco - as we whispered. Somewhere, perhaps deep in some Utah mountain holding nuclear waste, my discharge summary sits.

This baby's feet did drum, until we gave him calcium.

Over forty years, our emergency room morphed from a small, poorly lit, often doctorless corner to a sparkling twenty-million dollar center that was dedicated by President George H. W. Bush. But I do miss two things. Years ago, our hospital sponsored a rambunctious musical revue featuring hospital employees, doctors and a few civilians. This fundraiser is now a generic golf tournament. And, we no longer have as many in-house continuing education lectures. Early in my career, our education director, pediatrician and partner Dr. Lyman Page, would bring in guest lecturers from Boston. Today, you can dial up the University of Minnesota Pediatric Grand Rounds and see similar talks. This is enlightening, but you can't ask questions about children in your practice. I still enjoy showing my own medical slides. The interns and residents seem to enjoy them - only a few fall asleep.

CECIL

I first met Cecil when his mother brought him to see me because of poor grades. He was in 6th grade and had been an A student, but something had changed. His short term memory was failing. Cecil's mother recalled that one morning he searched and searched for his jacket while he was wearing it. Failure in school is usually related to psychological, social, or learning problems. But every now and the problem has a medical cause. In my first years in practice, I encountered two children who could not pay attention and were ultimately were diagnosed with brain abscesses. Epilepsy and brain tumors have presented themselves in a similar fashion. Almost forty years later Mrs. W remembered that the school counselor suggested she take Cecil to see that new young doctor in Saco.

Cecil's initial examination was normal but his responses seemed slow and he fumbled for words. Since his symptoms were sudden, I ordered an electro-encephalogram, which measures brain waves. Cecil's tracing showed disorganized waves with excessively high voltage. My initial diagnosis was temporal lobe epilepsy. But, I was wrong.

At the medical center, Cecil's spinal fluid evaluation was suggestive of measles slow virus disease or more specifically subacute sclerosing panenecphalitis (SSPE).

How does SSPE develop? The child first contracts measles at young age, which is fortunately rare today because of the measles vaccine. In some children the virus changes its genome and goes asleep deep within the brain, only to reactivate years later. When it does awake, the mutant virus goes amok, causing severe brain damage and often mimicking epilepsy.

Despite some success with anticonvulsants, Cecil was not able to return to school. His condition deteriorated and he needed supervision. There was no specific treatment available. Swallowing became a problem. The parents were salt of the earth Mainers. The father had a good manufacturing job in South Portland and his insurance was excellent.

I was always tardy for house calls. One weekend, as I opened the door, Mrs. W cheerfully hailed me. "Dr. Moore. If I'm ever convicted and sentenced to death, I want you as my executioner. You'll never show up." We tearfully discussed Cecil's downward spiral. Despite visiting nurses, Cecil's illness began to severely impact the family. He had increasing difficulty swallowing. I gently told Mrs. W that someday she would "have to part" with Cecil, words that she remembered forty years later.

One morning Cecil suddenly stopped talking and stared at the ceiling. He had spoken his last words, and it was time for the hospital. Just at that time I was reading of a bizarre case in a well-respected medical journal. A comatose Maine child was rushed to a Boston hospital. She was thought to have fulminating multiple sclerosis. Despite vigorous treatment the youngster died; autopsy revealed SSPE. She was Cecil's cousin.

They had measles together at the age of one. Mrs. W had told me this but I had never really believed the story.

Shame on me. Familial SSPE has been reported in siblings, one of identical twins, and cousins - but the these cases are very rare. This phenomenon suggests a possible inherited genetic susceptibility towards developing SSPE.

I contacted the cousin's Boston neurologist. Just at this time, we had replaced Cecil's nasal tube with a tube through the skin connecting his stomach to the outside world. We could drip in liquid feedings. The neurologist kindly came to Maine and consulted with us. He suggested administering an antiviral drug, Isoprinosine, via the gastrostomy tube. It held some promise with similar patients. Cecil's parents agreed to this treatment, and we were all hopeful. Initially there was some benefit, but after awhile the disease slowly progressed.

Cecil's insurance company made an effort to move Cecil into a high skill nursing home, but these centers never had the staff or environment to adequately care for him. He always wound up back in our hospital. When I was training in Cincinnati, we were we blessed to have a convalescent hospital for children. A wealthy family had bequeathed a mansion to the hospital, and it had been converted into a medical home for a range of disabled children. There was a full complement of physical and occupational therapists. The hospital was staffed by pediatric nurses and residents. Many years ago we had the opportunity to convert a local hospital into such a convalescent unit, but the bond failed. Recently, a Maine non-profit organization providing hospice care to children had to close due to loss of funding.

Cecil's family and I became close friends. Years later, his younger sister remembers coming home from school and seeing the ambulance in her driveway as Cecil was taken to the hospital. But she also recalls coming to our house at Christmas to view Wendy's gingerbread house. Mrs. W further adds that I told her of receiving a note from school that one of my sons was "very smart and college material." Apparently I sent a terse message back to his teacher - " if he's so smart, how come he has lost two pair of mittens already this winter?"

I treated Cecil's medical illnesses with small doses of garden variety medications. A little bit of penicillin for pneumonia, Pedialyte for diarrhea. Cecil always got better. He had the heart and lungs of an ox. The nurses grew very attached. They would mention his name years afterwards.

Cecil died quietly in his sleep, in the hospital, seven years after his admission. Today there is still no cure for SSPE. Newer drugs may slow progression but 95% of children contracting SSPE will succumb within five years of their first symptoms. The best treatment is prevention. Numerous studies have shown that children immunized against measles will not catch measles or develop SSPE. As an added benefit, widespread immunization will drastically reduce the amount of natural measles in the community. As a result, those too young to receive vaccine, like Cecil and his cousin, are unlikely to contract measles from the community.

I learned much about patience, perseverance, and loyalty from Cecil and his family.

72

ALL ABOARD

A young child with listlessness and a fever was carried to see me in the early 1970s from an adjacent community. She had the classical signs of meningitis, which is a deadly infection of the brain covering. This scary illness was always a great concern, until later vaccines almost completely eradicated this threat. Speed of treatment was critical. Ill children arriving in office would often have their spinal tap and antibiotics before being sent to the hospital.

One of the first effective meningitis treatments was a combination of three different antibiotics – an awkward program fraught with side effects. Then in 1961, ampicillin, a jazzed-up penicillin derivative, was formulated. It was something of a miracle cure for meningitis. I had used it to treat several sick children during my training. There was neither an intensive care unit nor infectious disease specialist at the medical center. I admitted the sleepy child to our local hospital and the nurses administered the ampicillin intravenously every six hours. To everyone's delight, our patient made a slow but steady recovery.

Her father was an engineer for the Maine Central Railroad. To express his gratitude, he offered my two eldest sons and me a real freight train ride. We would head northwest from Portland over gently rolling farmland to Fabyan, New Hampshire, on the far side of the White Mountains. This right of way was constructed from 1867 to 1875 as part of the Portland & Ogdensburg Railroad which connected the Atlantic Ocean and the Great Lakes. The project was a colossal engineering feat and spurred other similar under-takings in the western United States. The gem of this division is the Frankenstein Trestle which is 500 feet long, 80 feet high, and traverses a 4 degree curve.

The line to Lake Ontario proved unprofitable and traffic was routed north through St. Johnsbury, then finally to Montreal. Various mergers and bankruptcies followed and the line was abandoned several years after our trip. Many of these tracks have been converted to trails for biking and walking. Others remain in place as the Conway Scenic Railroad, which is a spectacular trip through Crawford Notch.

The tandem diesels rolled and lurched slowly upward. We waved at families gathered in backyards and at crossings. They knew the schedule.

The trip through Crawford Notch was mesmerizing, with views that are not available by foot or by automobile. The roadbed was prone to washouts and snow slides and plowing equipment was kept on sidings. The railroad ran parallel to the highway but high up on the mountainside. The sound of the engines echoed off the granite cliffs. There were major hiking trails that crossed our path and Christopher would blow the whistle so we wouldn't run anyone over. We could see Mount Washington in the near distance. The wives met us at the top of the notch, near Bretton Woods. We all drove back home after forcibly removing the boys, who wanted the engineer to drive the freight straight to Montreal. It was like a Make-a-Wish trip for two healthy children.

**Pictured: Christopher and Michael Moore
Maine Central Railroad**

PERCY'S DRUGSTORE

In 1968 Percy's Pharmacy was family owned and run and the unofficial hub of the community. At breakfast, across the Formica counter, a citizen could give and receive the latest information on marriages, infidelity, real estate taxes, sports teams, sewer systems and much, much more. The pharmacists also were very helpful in obtaining special drugs and formulae - and even made an occasional home delivery. The day that Percy's was sold to a chain, the doom and gloom was palpable. They ripped out the dining counter and replaced it with displays. But you could now buy guns, ammo, and liquor on Sundays. It was the harbinger of big box shopping. Today you can purchase live lobsters at the Walgreen's in Portland.

I usually took breakfast at Percy's when Wendy and the boys were visiting her parents on the West Coast. Graduate degrees were of no importance, and I was treated just like everyone else. Wendy once had a cranky conservative councilman paged at the counter. She wished to oppose his support for the elimination of kindergarten during tight economic times. He had to leave his breakfast and talk in public on the pharmacy phone.

My favorite conversation in Percy's took place as we were starting rehearsals for our biannual hospital musical. A New York production company would hit town and create a musical show using local doctors, nurses, and ordinary town wannabe stars. The hospital received the profits. One year a skit featured a group of physicians in drag. This required a costume. My friend Bobby was the pharmacist on duty. The scene went like this –

"Hey Bobby, help me."

"What is it, Doc?"

"Well," I yelled from three aisles over. "I'm here in front of the panty-hose display. I can't decide if I would look good in Earth Tone. Also, my size is exactly between Queen and petit King. What do you think, Bobby?"

"Whatever," he casually replied, as half a dozen customers swiveled their necks to stare at us.

The pendulum may be swinging back. After being sold to successive drug chains, the store is now owned locally in association with a community pharmacy group that sponsors a small fleet of stores throughout the state. I do think that chain and supermarket pharmacies do provide a service to the community. They offer convenience to those with cars. But the community pharmacies do an excellent job by offering downtown service to the elderly and disabled who often lack transportation. Maybe I can get them to restore the lunch counter.

UNDER THE GUN

The first bullet shattered the silence of a warm spring night and lodged into the side of an adjacent apartment. Our ward nurse leaned her pregnant body out of the hospital window.

"Sounds like a backfire," she wondered.

"No, no, no – that's gunfire," I said softly as I gently put my arm around her full waist and lowered her to the floor.

Several more bullets were fired in a random pattern.

"Are you sure?"

"Yes. They teach us that in medical school."

The only other time I worried about coming under fire was during my pediatric residency in Cincinnati at the time of the Martin Luther King riots. One night during the height of the disorder, my next-door neighbor's child became ill. Kathy's psychiatrist father Jim was out of town. She had a high fever, stiff neck and sported a surgically placed brain shunt due to excess spinal fluid at birth. She was now eight, and her shunt had never been revised or given her any problems. I was concerned about an infection and the possibility of meningitis.

The police and National Guard were keeping certain avenues open to Children's Hospital. After checking with the ER, we started out. I could hear sporadic gun fire in the distance. Earlier in the day I had watched in amazement as the house staff at the neighboring General Hospital sat transfixed, watching the Six Day Arab-Israeli War on TV. They were oblivious to the local militia in armored vehicles rumbling by in the street below.

I asked Kathy to get down low in her seat and stay below window level. About halfway to the hospital I was second-guessing myself. What do I tell Jim if we take a few bullets to the VW Beetle? We eventually arrived safely. Luckily it turned out to be a virus and Allison did well.

Back at our Maine hospital, we kept low and wheeled several infant and toddler cribs into the interior of the hospital. Would the parents of these children watch this drama on TV news at 11 from home?

The scene reminded me of the story told me by an intern from Puerto Rico at the Andrews Air Force Hospital. As a medical student, he and some buddies had gone to Havana for the weekend to try their luck at the casinos. They became somewhat incapacitated tasting the local rum and just made it back to the hotel room. The group awoke in mid morning to discover that the Castro liberation forces had blown out most of the room wall and they were looking through a gaping hole out into bright Caribbean daylight. They had slept through the whole battle. The fledgling doctors were able to reach the street using a fire escape that was barely attached to the hotel.

Local gun stories abound. As I returned back from a

weekend summer trip, my next-door neighbor boasted that his marksmanship had solved my woodchuck garden problem. I asked, "when?" and "wasn't discharging ammo within the city limits frowned upon?" My friend replied "bottom of the seventh inning" and "I didn't hear anything."

Michael and a friend were deer hunting sixty miles north of town. Flushing a deer from a cul de sac, anticipation turned to terror as a black bear charged from the woods. The buddy's last shot splintered the beast's rib into its heart and deposited it at their feet. Later that evening, with the conquered animal in the truck bed, the hunters cruised the narrow streets of the Old Port - as Saturday night college revelers oohed and aahed. There was the rumor that black-market bear gallbladders commanded a high price in the Asian market, but we won't go there. This vignette is retold every Christmas. Each year the bear becomes larger and the distance shorter.

The pediatric ward was a blur. After quickly relocating the children to safety, I was able to view the battlefield from a hospital window that seemed to be out of the line of fire. The sniper was hold up on the second floor of an apartment, shooting a target at right angles to the hospital. The police had cordoned off Route 1 and deployed sharpshooters behind several large oak trees.

Random shots continued to punctuate the night. In recalling this story my mind jumps back twenty years, to when I became a member a local Army Reserve medical unit. If there were funds remaining at the end of the year, we would drill with live M16s on the range.

When my targets were evaluated, it was decided that if the Russians ever invaded York County, I would be the last line of defense.

The police were unsuccessfully trying to lob tear gas canisters into the apartment through a screened-in second floor porch. I overheard plans to obtain multiple units of blood from the Red Cross in Portland. My Jeep was sitting quietly in the parking lot below, not going anywhere for a while.

After about an hour, the SWAT team stormed up a side stairway and exchanged fire with the shooter. The whole event seemed surreal. Incredibly, no one was hit and the team retreated. Finally, about an hour later the tear gas assault was successful and the battle over. The rifleman was a distraught teenager who had enough ammo, food and water to spend his summer vacation firing off rounds. There were no injuries.

The next day one of the office nurses asked me if I had seen the event on late night TV news.

"Yea. It looked pretty tense," I replied.

Pictured: Pediatric Ward, Webber Hospital 1970's

TIES THAT BIND

When we entered medical school, Dean Syvertsen only had three rules for us. The first was that we would will always be seen in coat and tie. Number two mandated that during the day we would be either in class or in the infirmary. Lastly there would be one warning and this was it. We often studied in official garb. On the undergraduate campus we were instantly identified as medical students or someone running for class office. Clip-on bow ties were acceptable.

Many years later novelty ties would become my trademark. My first job each morning was to pick a tie to match the season or holiday or sports event and my mood and the weather. My shirt colors, usually stripes, had to be complementary. Then, the whole ensemble had to pass Wendy's muster before I left for work.

My first was the Snoopy tie. It was solid with little tiny figures of Snoopy in a scrub suit woven into the background. I purchased the Snoopy tie from a local emergency room doctor whose father manufactured them for a pediatric surgical group. It announced that I was a non-threatening soul who worked with children and might be a doctor. Airline staff always noticed. I was always hoping for an upgrade, but it was usually an extra Coke or pretzels.

My buffalo tie was sent by grateful vacationing parents from upstate New York. The family had visited several area hospitals because of their child's high fever, but without a diagnosis. A nurse in our emergency room obtained a urine sample, which proved to be infected.

The dozen ferocious bison, charging across my tie, always gave me energy for the day.

Another family, needing a doctor while visiting in Bermuda, called me. Having some contacts there, I was able to help. As a thank you, they bought me sailboat tie from Trimingham's in Hamilton. It seemed to evoke tranquility when I wore it.

When traveling out of state, my lobster ties often provoked comment, perhaps because the small size of the crustaceans made them look head lice. It is now for the most part forbidden to accept pharmaceutical company gifts. In the past I envisioned small parasite logos, like bedbugs or pinworms, on the tie, along with the name of the proper drug for cure. Apparently there are new antibacterial ties featuring pictures of different bacteria.

Peanuts and Muppet ties are invariably popular for all seasons, sports, and holidays. College, medical school, and organization ties were pricey, bland, and difficult to clean, more suited for a Wall Street broker than a baby doctor.

A physician friend and his wife adopted a toddler from China. When K was nine or ten she brought me a Sponge Bob tie from Wal-Mart. She felt it would make me appear as a younger and cooler pediatrician. It has helped in situations outside the office, especially schools, to help break the ice with children who don't know me.

Bear ties also are plentiful: Yogi bear, Pooh Bear, U of

Maine Black Bear, the Similac Bear, Smoky Bear to name just some. The combination of Teddy Bears, drums, and bugles always sends cold shivers my way. This trio would not only appear on ties, but could also be found gaily decorating the prescriptions a certain staff doctor when I was a resident physician. His young patients were often admitted late at night. These children and their parents, along with the nurses and resident doctors, were never happy. I would often be on my way to nap in the doctor's lounge when I would fleetingly glimpse the little drums and bugles in the hand of the newly arriving mother. It was like seeing flashing blue lights in your rear view mirror.

Jessi gave me a Christmas tie with a musical chip containing three carols. Sometimes for fun I would wear the tie in July and press the chip as I walked through the emergency room. Another time I feared some grave neurological disease in a six month infant who was rhythmically rotating his head while sitting in his mother's lap. Only after several minutes did I realize that the infant was just following the pendulum path of my new tie that sported half a dozen yellow smiley faces :).

More frequently I see physicians who only occasionally care for children, wearing pediatric novelty ties. I am reluctant to question them. There have also been some studies that incriminate ties as disease –carrying accessories. I would frequently tuck my tie in when examining infants during flu season. Bow ties may be more hygienic, but lack the surface area to fully display colors and animals. In truth there are numerous conflicting studies regarding both the ability of doctor's clothing to carry germs and a family's preference for formal or informal physician garb. But a recent study showed that doctors who treat the oldest and the youngest are the happiest in their profession.

SEWING LESSONS

A female pediatrician, now an author, watched her first surgery in medical school. She commented that it appeared no more difficult than the childhood sewing skills taught to her by her mother. But despite narcotic lollipops and Valium like nasal spray for sedation, we often have to suture a moving target.

My second summer in Maine I was alone in the office one Saturday afternoon. A mother from Massachusetts brought in her daughter with a long facial laceration caused by a piece of metal. The wound was clean and not deep, but extended down from the eye onto the check. We had no plastic surgeons available. I was it. Mother, of course, was a nurse.

The suturing went well, as the girl was quite cooperative. The Novocain did its job and everyone stayed calm. We took a few breaks. I was able to close the wound with fifteen delicate sutures. Between a female facial laceration and the registered nurse mother, I sweated every stitch. It took me half an hour. When I finished the edges matched perfectly. The mother was given written instructions and asked to come back in three days. I wished to begin the early removal of alternate sutures to prevent crosshatch scarring.

They were a no show. I called the motel. Mother and child had checked out. There was no answer in Massachusetts. Finally, after ten days of detective work, I contacted my new nurse friend at her home.

"Dr. Moore. I forgot to call you. We took the long way home. I took the stitches out with my nail clipper."

"You what?"

"Don't worry, Dr. Moore. I sterilized it with alcohol."

"How does it look?"

"Great. The cut stayed closed. No infection. I have a friend who is a plastic surgeon. He'll follow up. Thanks again."

I used to carry a suture set in my football bag. It was used three or four times. Once, a school bus was my halftime operating theater. My patient was an opposing player with a split chin. His teammates crowded around to watch. Some were startled as I handed drapes and iodine swabs to my new assistants. Questions came from the back of the crowd. The procedure went well. The coach was not happy, however, as the players ignored his intermission pep talk.

My football bag was used again one Sunday morning. Friends, with varying carpentry skills, were helping my neighbor construct pool decking. Suddenly, Joe took a hammer to the head and produced an even bloodier Mary. A trip to the local ER for gash repair would have greatly delayed the project. Despite numerous suggestions about my suturing technique, I was able to persevere. In retrospect, only one volunteer, a former Navy corpsman, had any past medical experience.

Late one afternoon a good friend brought his son to the

office for a laceration above the right eye. My patient did fine, but father became a progressively delicate shade of lime green. He was standing just inside the bathroom which had a linoleum floor.

"Craig, please lie down. Now. Use the carpet."

"I'll be OK, doctor. I'm a volunteer fireman."

SPLAT. Craig led with his chin just inside the bathroom. Now both father and son had identical injuries. When the twin trauma was repaired, I called his house. My voice was recognized.

"What are you guys doing? It's been three hours", questioned his wife Betsy.

Another time a mother brought in her school aged daughter with a small horizontal forehead laceration. It was tucked neatly into a skin crease. If I used 7-0 eye suture the scar would be invisible. I started to explain. Mother was rightly upset and the conversation went thusly-

"I don't want a rinky dink job, Dr. Moore. I want a plastic surgeon."

"No problem, " I answered, having been in this situation before. But I needed to work quickly since the wound had to be closed within a few hours. There would be at least an hour car ride to the specialist - they were all in Portland.

I retired to the phone and called a plastic surgeon's office. The situation delicately explained to the secretary.

"Well doctor, we are VERY busy this week. We could see your patient a WEEK from Thursday at 1 PM. Would that be OK?"

Finally, not too long ago, I went to a plastic surgeon for a hand problem. Unknowingly, I entered the wrong door and walked into the cosmetic surgery section. I could read the look on the receptionist's face as she fumbled for the words to gently explain that I was beyond repair.

EARLY ARRIVALS

In the early 1900's the care of premature infants was defaulted to the obstetricians, meaning that babies weighing less than two pounds were wrapped and left in a corner of the delivery room to die. Although obstetricians pioneered the use of incubators for preemies, they had scant time to supervise their care. Hospitals had little financial incentive to devote resources to small newborns, especially when treatment was primitive. In 1941 my mother delivered premature twins in the suburbs of New York. My father was dispatched to the city to procure special formula. By the time he returned, they had both succumbed. Today, they would have certainly survived.

Gradually, pediatricians gained entry to the nursery. The baby boom after World War II drove improvements in newborn care. Supplemental oxygen reduced cerebral palsy in preemies, but at the price of damage to the developing retina, which sometimes led to blindness. The Scandinavians developed machines that, using a few drops of blood, could analyze the level of a baby's oxygen, allowing for more precise regulation. Today the same information can be obtained by a meter that simply clips onto a finger or toe.

Temperature regulation is critical to newborn treatment. Doctors originally attempted to keep preemies cool, with predictably disastrous results. The invention of the Isolette, a Plexiglas box with ports for access, allowed for better observation and temperature control of the infant. Performing a spinal tap or starting an IV through the ports was like building a ship in a bottle. There was an iron-clad rule during my training that the Isolette top was not to be swung all the way back unless there was a dire emergency. Residents violated this rule at their peril, as the senior pediatrician would sneak up behind the offender and slam the top back down onto his knuckles.

Towards the end of the 1960s, infrared infant warmers, just like the ones that keep your fast food burger warm, became available. This advancement allowed full access to warm babies especially useful during resuscitations. Tall nurses and bald pediatricians often found themselves overheated by these lamps. Also during this time, the treatment of yellow jaundice with blue or white fluorescent light became popular, reducing the need for blood exchange transfusions. Large newborn units with enough blue bilirubin lights turned on looked like nightclubs.

Until the medical center finally opened a neonatal intensive care unit in the 1970s, our small band of pediatricians would ride ambulances to collect babies in distress from smaller hospitals in our county. I would hold my breath as we entered the nursery, hoping for at least a slightly pink baby. The ambulance trips always seemed to be over dark, icy roads. Even when the ICU was opened, a dedicated neonatal transport ambulance was years away.

At that time, respiratory distress syndrome (RDS) was still the primary killer of preemies. These infants often lack lung surfactant, a chemical compound that keeps the air sacks open. A crude, but fairly accurate test was the double bubble challenge. We would suction amniotic fluid from the baby's stomach at birth, mix it with alcohol in a test tube and then watch the interface. A double row of bubbles indicated adequate surfactant. Lesser bubbles meant immature lungs and a rapid trip north to the newborn specialists at the medical center. The test took two minutes to perform, with all the immediacy and adrenaline of a slot machine.

It was discovered that the administration of steroids to mothers prior to early delivery might modify or prevent RDS. Over the years, treatment progressed over the years from watchful waiting with oxygen mask, to hours of hand ventilation, and finally to the gold standard of breathing machines. At long last, artificial surfactant became available. This wonder drug could be squirted into preemie lungs right after birth, and it worked. I remember two newborn x-rays that Dr. Mary Ellen Avery, Chief of Boston Children's Hospital, had hand-carried back from Japan. The first RDS film looked like chest snowstorm. An hour later, after homemade Japanese surfactant had been sprayed, the x-ray and baby were normal.

A few years after my arrival, the nurses in our local hospital nursery achieved the outstanding benchmark of only eight newborn deaths per thousand deliveries – felt to be the absolutely lowest rate achievable by a community hospital. We were all very proud.

In 1987 the Academy of Pediatrics introduced its Neonatal Resuscitation Program (NRP). This protocol set standards for the treatment of depressed newborns. The course included a detailed manual, hands on practice, and both paper and practical exams.

Although I took the course at least a half dozen times, there was always a bit of nervousness when the exam sheet was collected. Too many SAT memories. The NRP was responsible for the intact survival of several babies born without heartbeats at our hospital. Eventually the NRP spread to countries worldwide.

Today our nurses can evaluate sick newborns, breathe for them, start intravenous lines, and give drugs – while awaiting the doctor. The list of newborn advances goes on and on – fetal ultrasound, intrauterine surgery, neonatal surgery, genetic testing. The golden era of newborn medicine is indeed upon us.

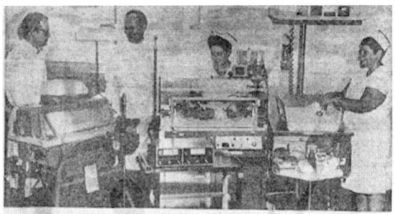

Intensive Care Unit Aids Infants

Pictured: Dr. Moore, Dr. Maurice Ross, Carrie Whittemore, RN
and Joyce Lyons, RN
Circa 1970

GOD BLESS YOU

There is a strong French-Canadian presence in Maine, and their Catholic Church has played a prominent role in the healing of local children.

"Dr. Moore, Sister wants to see you in microbiology. Now."

I thanked the ward nurse and headed downstairs. It was always reassuring having a nun as the microbiologist back then. The bacteria were always correctly identified and the report written in neat cursive handwriting. I once praised a nurse friend for her beautiful parochial-school script. "That's just half of it", she sighed. "I started out left-handed. The nuns had another plan for me."

"Dr. Moore. Thank you for coming down. We are growing a strange bacteria out of the blood culture that was drawn last night from the new baby in the nursery. It appears to be a streptococcus. I typed it and it seems to a group B. I've never seen it infecting a newborn before. It could be a contaminant, but it grew rather quickly. I should probably work it up and do antibiotic sensitivities. Is that all right?"

Back at the hospital, I took the nun's advice and treated the newborn with antibiotics for a full seven days. Unknown to us, we were on the crest of a wave of group B streptococcal infections in nurseries around the nation. The disease is contracted from the cervix during labor and delivery. There were newborn deaths across the country. Today pregnant women receive cervical cultures at thirty-seven weeks and are given antibiotics during labor if they carry this streptococcus. This program has served us well, but years ago, it was Sister's astute diagnosis that saved a life.

Decades ago, nuns ran a small hospital, Notre Dame, on the road to Biddeford Pool. It served the French population well and was a haven for summer visitors from Quebec.

A diabetic Canadian child had been rushed to their emergency room. By phone I told the Sisters to send the child and family up the road to our larger community hospital, and that I would the meet parents there. Just as I was about to wrap up these instructions, I got my comeuppance.

"Dr. Moore, here's the blood work. The child has acidosis, needs insulin, and we also have started an intravenous line. Please order the insulin dose and fluid rate. We will be admitting the child here. We have the skills to do this. This family from Quebec will be more comfortable speaking in French. We will expect you shortly. Thank you."

I did this and the child recovered because of their excellent care. Later, when the hospital became a skilled nursing facility, the Sisters cared for terminally ill children with a compassion that would rival any hospice program in the country. In the adjacent St. Andre's Home, unwed pregnant teens from all over Maine would live and study while awaiting childbirth. The girls were not generally dropouts but often high school students who would go on to college or nursing school after giving their babies up for adoption. Because of their age any non-obstetrical medical issues were handled by the pediatricians. I got to know many of them well. They were the kind of teens who would stay in touch with Christmas cards and graduation announcements. The Sisters did an outstanding job of supporting the girls' mental and physical health.

Religious themes appeared elsewhere on my daily watch. Sick newborns might have religious medals in their cribs or pinned to hospital tops. My senior partner, Dr. Ross, related times when despite his best efforts a baby would not respond to treatment. He might then call for a specific elderly priest. I had noted an old cloudy bottle of *holy water* on the nursery shelf - tucked among the antibiotics. On several occasions the intervention was successful.

Father John's Save the Baby cough syrup was also available. The product not only invoked Church blessings but foretold of possible pneumonia if not purchased and used liberally.

I remember a one week old infant who was brought in for a routine follow-up. He was healthy but for a small hole between the two ventricular pumping chambers of the heart, which was would probably heal itself in due course. In the hospital, mother seemed to understand that this defect was unlikely to progress into a serious condition.

On arrival the baby was a bit mottled from the slightly cold air in the exam room. The mother bundled him up as I left briefly to answer a phone call from the hospital.

The new mother had mistaken her baby's slightly blue hue for a terminal event, left the exam room, and called a local priest from our waiting room phone. When I arrived back from my prolonged phone call, I found the clergyman administering last rites to the healthy infant.

I later reassured my families in the waiting room.

I'D RATHER BE LUCKY THAN SMART

My pediatrician son has an oft-repeated phrase, perhaps true both in medicine and life - "I'd rather be lucky than smart." However, many writer's manuals caution against the overvaluation of chance. Chance occurrences happen to us every day. Perhaps they are important only if they lead to significant outcomes. Many pundits, including Louis Pasteur, feel that chance only benefits the prepared mind - maybe excluding lottery winners. Or perhaps there is a higher power involved. Here are a few stories from my forty years. You be the judge.

As I arrived at the hospital one blustery April morning, the Wells town ambulance came roaring into the emergency room entrance with all lights flashing. I stepped out of my Scout.

"Hey Doc," yelled the paramedic. "We need you to pronounce one of the kids in the back. A lobsterman found them both hanging onto a capsized catamaran in the harbor. Don't know how long they were in the water. I think his buddy is OK."

My mouth becomes dry and my pulse races. The paramedic's euphemism brings to mind all the words we use to dance around dead patients – passed, didn't make it, gone to heaven, etc. I think of all the parents to whom I have told this news, and how they sobbed. Lastly, I think of how cold the ocean water would be in April, which is a winter month in Maine.

Years later, I recalled this scene as two friends and I

were sailing a cutter class boat up from Massachusetts to Maine in June. We were drinking strong coffee at 3 AM to keep awake during our two-hour watches. City lights and heat lightning sparkled to port and a faint yellow strip of dawn crept over the ocean horizon. I was wearing a Gortex top and bottom over jeans and a sweater, plus the obligatory winter gloves. I was just barely comfortable in early summer. How cold was the April ocean water for the two students?

Back at the hospital, I quickly scramble into the ambulance. Both boys appear to be in their late teens. One is moaning. The other is ashen and silent. I grab a stethoscope and yell " Clothes off ! This one may be OK!"

One would think that a diagnosis of death is straightforward - but historically there have been pitfalls. Early twentieth century caskets often contained internal bells with a tube snaking up to the outside world - allowing relatives to gather daily and listen for the chimes of a bogus demise. Even at the time of this catamaran mishap, EMT skills and monitors were primitive- often fostering a *scoop and run* attitude, paying scant attention to the patient. Fortunately, a groundswell of national concern soon led to advanced training and standards for ambulance professionals. However, even today, one can read newspaper accounts of startled patients awakening in the morgue.

Back in the ambulance entrance, I asked the attendant to silence the engine, allowing me to appreciate a faint and very slow heartbeat.

The first boater responded to minimal care.

His companion needed more rigorous treatment. We surrounded the victim with warm blankets and infused him with heated fluids. His intense shivering was treated with intravenous medications. There is a huge risk of cardiac ventricular fibrillation while rewarming, and we were lucky to avoid it. Today, a heart-lung bypass machine, if available, gives doctors pinpoint control over severely hypothermic patients.

Both students made full recoveries. The one who almost died sent me a note of gratitude. I replied that he should thank the lobsterman who had rescued them. They had been in forty degree water for an hour. This environment kills some people after thirty minutes. Was it the constitution of their young bodies, force of will, or just fate?

A mother in the practice was driving though northern Maine. Suddenly, she heard some gurgling from the rear seat. She looked around to see the lap belt wrapped around her son's neck. He was blue and just barely breathing.

She stopped, opened the door, and leaned on the horn. Just as the child was about to asphyxiate, a trucker rolled his rig to a stop, flew into the back seat, and with his knife cut the child free. He somehow got the toddler's breathing started, The ambulance arrived, and a three-hour observation in the emergency room followed. The warmth and security of an automobile can disappear in an instant, and I urge everyone to equip theirs with a comprehensive emergency kit.

One morning an ear, nose and throat physician and I entered the Air Force ER door together, exchanging small talk, just as a child stopped breathing. An intern had unknowingly placed a tongue blade against a critically infected airway. The ENT doctor skillfully passed a breathing tube by the obstruction while I started cardiac compressions. The child responded and went home undamaged several days later. Without the specialist, the outcome would have been different. Why was he there?

Years earlier I was giving a talk to my Air Force colleagues concerning summer pediatric problems. Since I was a "90 day military pediatric wonder" my formal training in caring for children was thin. I showed some slides of poison snakebites, toxic mushrooms, and then a quick mention of "handlebar pancreatitis". In this condition the biker falls onto a handlebar end without a rubber grip and bruises his pancreas. I have photos of two children branded with a circular purple bruise next to the umbilicus from such an injury. As I finished my tidbit, several captains in the back of the room started mumbling to each other, and then abruptly they left the room.

Since that time I have only twice seen or heard of a sudden physician exodus during a medical lecture. I once witnessed a small group of politically conservative pediatricians stage a walkout. They left the auditorium when a nationally known pediatrician began to praise the Medicare program and then promoted a single-payer plan for all children.

Another time, a bureaucratic physician was giving a

somewhat dry talk on government medical spending. It was Sunday morning in Seattle. Suddenly 'oohs and aahs' came from the audience. The speaker was pleased though somewhat puzzled. Finally the captive doctors jumped to their feet and stormed the podium. And then past it, towards the large picture window, as Mt. Helens erupted in the background.

Back at the air base hospital, neither politics nor geography was cause of the fleeing surgeons. As I was discussing bike pancreatitis, a child with that injury was being wheeled into the operating room. In this era before CT and sonograms, sometimes all a surgeon could do was open up an injured belly. But the Air Force doctors knew that this child did a have a bike injury and you don't want to do exploratory surgery on an injured pancreas. They postponed surgery and ordered pancreas enzymes. The lab tests were very high. The child was treated with intravenous fluids and rest. He slowly recovered. Luck or coincidence?

Christopher called me from Colorado with his typical salutation. "Here's one for you doc."

The patient in question was a pre-teen with a slurred voice, drooling and difficulty swallowing, mostly at night. Several specialists had been consulted with no diagnosis. The vocal cords looked normal. There was some question of a psychological problem.

"Jeez, that doesn't sound like an emotional problem", I replied.

103

"I know. I think I'll get a CT scan to look at the larynx."

"Sounds good to me."

The scan was ordered. But the tech made her first slice a bit higher than usual and accidently imaged some brain tissue. She was disturbed by something she saw in the cerebellum. It looked like a mass. She took more slices. It was an abnormal area.

The patient was sent to a children's hospital where a tumor was removed. The prognosis was good. The parents brought my son a bottle of wine a year later. The tumor would have eventually been found. But did the lucky slice improve the outlook?

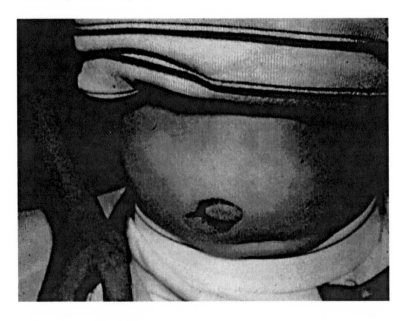

Pictured: Handlebar Pancreatitis

A DISEASE TOO SOON

"My husband died last year. He was 26. He had been in Vietnam. They sent him home because he couldn't fight anymore."

I was flying from Maine to Baltimore for a medical conference. In those days there was more conversation among fellow airline passengers.

The young woman next to me told me that her husband had developed a severe skin disease in Vietnam and had been sent back to the States. A specialist thought it might be lupus. He developed open sores and progression of the disease. Despite the efforts of the best military doctors, he eventually died. This grieving wife was considering nursing school and asked my advice.

We talked for almost an hour. She had shown courage and strength in caring for her husband. As the plane descended, we agreed that nursing would be a good fit.

Several years later, it suddenly dawned upon me that her husband may have died of Agent Orange disease. Agent Orange is a mixture of two phenoxy herbicides that was used as a military defoliant in Vietnam. It came in 55 gallon drums with orange stripes. The 2,4,5 T compound was often contaminated with dioxin. The role, if any, of Agent Orange in producing human disease is very controversial and beyond the scope of this chapter. However, the Agent Orange Act of 1991 concluded that there was sufficient evidence of an association between Agent Orange and soft tissue sarcomas as well as Hodgkin's and non-Hodgkin's lymphoma. It can also cause skin rashes and blistering. Over my forty years of practice I examined at least several thousand civilian males age 18 to 21. I never encountered a blistering skin rash that led to death. The Agent Orange connection seems too strong in this tragic case.

What other diseases have I seen too early?

A teenager was hospitalized with a high fever and a whole body, lobster-red rash. Despite antibiotics and intravenous fluids it was difficult to keep her blood pressure stable. Her cultures were negative for bacteria. Her total body glow was unlike anything we had ever seen.

Fortunately, she began to slowly improve. Pediatric patients usually have strong hearts and lungs free of smoke damage. They usually handle disease better than the very young or very old. She finally left the hospital without a firm diagnosis.

Several years later my partner passed me in the hall.

"Remember our friend with the unknown illness and rash ?"

"All too well, " I sighed.

"I just saw her for a sore throat. I asked her if she was using tampons at the time of her hospitalization. She said yes. I think she had toxic shock syndrome."

Toxic shock syndrome was initially described as a disease caused by staph bacteria growing on a foreign object such as super-absorbent tampons in a body cavity. The bacteria produce a toxin which causes a rash the color of a boiled lobster and drop in blood pressure. The illness was first fully described by Dr. James K. Todd, a Denver pediatrician, in 1978 -several years after our patient became ill. The seven children he described had staph on their mucous membranes but not in their blood. That suggested a toxin. There are still many unanswered questions about toxic shock syndrome. We now know that can occur in both sexes. A male teen patient of mine developed a case following nasal surgery despite the fact that a plastic splint was purposely used in place of cotton packing.

Another young child came to the office with a temperature of 105. His hemoglobin was 3 grams per 100 milliliters of blood. Normal is 11 or 12. Not good.

In a child, this combination of high fever and severe anemia is unfortunately a warning sign for leukemia. Further studies showed no signs of a white blood cell malignancy but turned up evidence of gastrointestinal bleeding. An x-ray demonstrated an ulcer in the duodenum - the part of the small bowel just past the stomach. Treatment with antacids and oral iron healed the erosion.

During my year of internship, our city hospital was crammed with patients of all ages who had peptic ulcer disease. Medical treatment was often ineffective. Even with aggressive surgery, patients sometime bled to death. What we did not know in the 1960s was that peptic ulcer disease was often caused by the H. pylori bacteria and could be treated with broad-spectrum antibiotics and acid blockers. If I had processed a large box of antibiotic pills and Prilosec (not available then) I could have been appointed Chief of Medicine somewhere.

The link between H. pylori bacteria and peptic ulcer disease was established by Dr. J. Robin Warren, a pathologist from Australia. He, too, saw a disease before its time by viewing strange bacteria in pathological specimens from ulcers in the usually sterile upper gastrointestinal tract. This link was doubted for decades. In 2005, Dr. Barry Marshall and Dr. Warren were awarded a Nobel Prize in Medicine- their theory belatedly accepted. In retro- spect I was lucky that my patient healed his ulcer with minimal treatment.

Before I came to Maine, my senior partner had a patient with all the signs of hemophilia. The child had been examined in Boston by a famous hematologist. The experts were unable to make a diagnosis of classic hemophilia. In 1952, British hematologists discovered a similar patient named Steven Christmas. His blood did not clot in the test tube when hemophilia A factor was added. Hence hemophilia B or Christmas disease. We now know that 15-20% of hemophilia patients have B disease. Our child had this illness before its discovery. Another B disease we saw too soon was the baby from another chapter with a group B streptococcal infection - months before this bacteria spawned a national epidemic.

Several other children in my practice may also have had

diseases before their time. I don't have enough proof but Lyme arthritis is on the list. It behooves physicians to report clusters or even individual cases of unusual aliments. They may even get the illness named after them.

PUMPING IRON

"Dr. Moore, this baby is getting yellower by the hour."

It was early evening and the nurse was concerned. The Rh-positive infant was about 12 hours old. Rh disease or hemolytic disease of the newborn (HDN), is a serious illness that damaged or killed thousands of babies in the last century. If a mother and her fetus have different Rh blood markers, the baby may develop severe jaundice at birth. This yellow pigment may stain the brain of the newborn causing deafness, cerebral palsy or death.

In 1968 a preventative treatment, Rhogan, became available. This particular infant just missed the Rhogan debut and he needed an exchange transfusion as soon as possible. In this procedure the newborn's blood is exchanged with banked blood, two teaspoons at a time. Fresh O Rh negative blood must be used. Older blood cannot be substituted.

We looked at the outdates on the O Negative blood on hand. None were usable. We needed a fresh donor, and quickly. Ten people were on the list, but nobody was home. There were no answering machines to tell us that Harry was at bingo. I was stumped.

It was then that someone at the nurse's station floated up the idea of PAYING emergency donors. Who was the last paid O Rh negative blood donor that I knew? Of course, it was myself.

In medical school I had been paid twenty five dollars per unit of freshly donated blood. That sum would buy two weeks of lunch in the hospital cafeteria. And, it was more pleasant than my other paid research job that involved swallowing feeding tubes.

"Please call the lab technician from the blood bank to draw a unit of blood from me - stat."

"I don't think they can do that, Dr. Moore."

"Why?" I asked.

"It sounds weird," she replied.

"What's the alternative?"

When the phlebotomist raised the same doubts, I played the *very sick baby* card again. All of the lab technicians had children of their own. My blood looked healthy as it filled the plastic bag. Our nurses did not hook me up directly to the baby, as they do in the black and white battlefield movies. The lab said my blood would be just fine.

The baby tolerated the procedure well with and the yellow faded quickly. He was discharged a few days later in good condition. My partners took a dim view of all this, but they never told me what they would have done. Hospital administrators looked for a rule that I had violated. They found none.

Recently Wendy noted that she too was once a nurse blood donor for her own sick patient. What a great question on the eHarmony.com compatibility questionnaire. "Have you ever donated a unit of blood and then administered it to a sick child? Would you like to meet someone who is also a donor/hanger?" It would be a good screening for compassion, ingenuity, squeamishness and health.

We were moving into our new hospital in 1979. Through the drizzle, ambulances transported the remaining patients from the old building a mile away. Only after the equipment was removed did we realize the shabby condition of the former hospital. I was one of three doctors who had voted not to build the new hospital but to renovate the old building. Fortunately we were outvoted.

Of course the grand opening of our new emergency room quickly attracted a very sick child. One hour after the ribbon was cut, a profoundly anemic infant arrived. The diagnosis was unclear but the need for an emergency transfusion was clear. But we did not yet have a pediatric pump that pushes thick donated blood cells through a tiny intravenous needle.

I stepped onto the shiny new pediatric unit and tried to reassure the anxious parents. We hung the blood bag from an intravenous pole. Only a few drops fell very slowly from the filter. At this rate it would take hours to stabilize the infant. Then I remembered words from my first ski instructor - "Let gravity be your friend!"

The nurses grafted a few poles together. With every added foot in height, the packed cells dripped a bit faster. Finally, I climbed a stepladder, pushed aside a square of acoustical tile, and gently lifted the bag into the false ceiling among the pipes and electrical conduits. The nursing staff cheered as the blood dripped even faster just as the CEO, board of directors, and TV crew came around the corner and onto the new wing. Sharp words were exchanged concerning the alteration of hospital property. We finally agreed to an informal truce so that our differences did not appear on the eleven o'clock news. Everyone became less irritable as the baby's condition improved.

THREE SECOND DIAGNOSES

The concept was first introduced during a medical school coffee break. Our preceptor was the late Dr. Harry Savage, who had been a general practitioner in upstate New Hampshire until heath issues caused him to take a position at the medical school. But he had also been a judge and mayor. Legend has it that "Harry's Boys" often fared well with their traffic tickets.

"Boys, there are two instant diagnoses that will help pay for medical school debt. First is when the patient feels the xiphoid process (that pointy piece that hangs down from the breastbone - yes, that's it) while in the shower, and runs to your office. Second is when people pee green during asparagus season."

Dr. Savage was spot on. When a child arrives with a bizarre-looking small rash or spot, my first order of business is to see if it wipes off with a swipe of an alcohol pad. A choking toddler may have a blade of grass lodged in the back of the throat. I will add to the list.

Radial head subluxation is a pediatric malady only seen in children under four. When the arm is pulled up suddenly, the top of the radius bone may pop of out the fibrous ring that holds it place. The elbow locks and becomes painful. A two-second maneuver pops it back in. All pediatric offices are aware of "nursemaid's elbow." But to the crying toddler and frightened parents, the doctor appears as the ultimate miracle worker.

Twice during my pediatric training ill children lurched down the emergency room corridor struggling with four or five full 8 ounce glass urine bottles - allowing me to make the call of undiagnosed diabetes in several seconds from twenty feet.

Like afternoon tea, a rapid spot diagnosis picks me up for a few hours.

Another diagnosis took a bit longer than three seconds but not more than a minute. The baby had a murmur. But the cardiogram showed that her heart electricity flowed north not south like normal infants. I was like the power company meter reader. This finding could only mean a heart problem called a cushion defect – a low hole between the heart's two receiving chambers. Cardiac catheterization confirmed the suspicion.

I once divined that a woman kept pigs.

"How did you know that, Dr. Moore?"

The mother had brought in a worm that her child had passed. The parasite was resting quietly in a glass jar. It looked like a garden worm. I confessed to mother that I had seen this once before.

I was initially puzzled because standard teaching was that the human roundworm is only passed from human to human. Moreover, parasite eggs don't survive under two feet of frozen snow. Through the magic of the Internet I had discovered several cases of pig to human transmission reported from Europe. About that time I stopped using pig manure in my garden compost bin, just to be on the safe side.

I astounded the parents of a son with severe hives and wheezing when I made the rapid diagnosis of a llama-induced allergic reaction. I first established the family had no pets at home. Then I fessed up that I had noticed the fluorescent, freshly- applied "Wild Animal Farm" sticker pasted over his heart.

Another time close friends brought their son through the back door. Eric had nasty purple hemorrhages all around his mouth. His parents feared a contagious disease or a nasty blood problem. I evaluated the situation while standing in the door frame.

"Eric, have you been sucking on a drinking glass while watching TV?"

"Yes, Dr. Moore."

"Please don't do that again. You're scaring your parents. Thank you."

BREAKING UP IS HARD TO DO

"Hey, Dr. Moore, these family folders aren't working anymore."

I will always remember the day I heard these words from my secretary. For several years after my arrival in Maine all the children's medical charts would neatly nest inside their Smith or Cote family folder, snuggled right together. This allowed us to view the child in the context of family. But shared custody and out-of-wedlock births soon challenged our tidy system. Luckily, many of my staff had laser memories and could recite these tangled family trees by memory. Today, the click of a mouse can unscramble these complex relationships.

Growing up, divorce seemed to be a rare event. In most states you had to prove infidelity with photos of a real tryst at a hotel. If the split was mutually agreeable, some couples actually staged these "affairs". I remember the weekend that a lawyer friend from New York spent with us in 1970. He was in near-constant phone contact with private detective Greenberg, who was hiding in the bushes on Cape Cod watching a cottage for signs of sin.

Wendy and her office colleagues soon learned to spot signs of an impending divorce. A stay-at-home mom would suddenly get a job on the outside. Other separations were triggered by a pregnancy. Was a wedding ring out for repairs, taken off during a home project or absent for a more ominous reason? Sometimes a seemingly perfect couple with beaming

119

offspring would split up, and conversely, we saw numerous couples who seemed to be horribly mismatched on the surface, last for decades.

College settings always seemed to illuminate divorce. One of my sons commented that he may have been the only freshman in his dorm without step-siblings. Wendy noted that some of my college classmates had different partners at reunions over the years. When I turned fifty, my alumni magazine began to publish an alarming number of photos featuring classmates holding young infants who were not their grandchildren. There was usually a quote such as "I now have the time to be the good father that I never was." There was never a rebuttal from the first wife.

After getting divorced, some parents would communicate only through their lawyers. Other former spouses and their new partners, plus both extended families, would all gather for a massive weekly dinner. One father demanded that I call him personally after every visit from his ex-wife and child. It was often difficult to follow court rulings regarding which guardian had current medical decision-making power. Recently a grandmother vetoed an H1N1 booster as unnecessary.

No parents ever painted a black line down the center of the house or chain-sawed the dwelling in two, but living arrangements generated the most acrimony. Many children were subjected to joint custody and the grind of moving to a different home twice a week. Perhaps the best plan involved the *parents* rotating through the house with the children staying put.

The medical economics of dealing with divorced families was often challenging. Still-wounded moms would often flip the bill at the receptionist on the way out with a curt "send the bill to his *father*". If the father had disappeared, was unemployed, or had no insurance, his abandoned family would qualify for Medicaid – "that new insurance that covers everything". One of the most thoughtful programs involved a father who had moved to Florida. He set up a medical and dental checking account in that state. Mother had the checkbook in Maine and father received the bank statements to monitor the spending. His faith and good will was rewarding to everyone involved.

GOOD IDEAS GONE BAD

Brand new in the 1970's, MAX was hailed as the latest high tech device for cardiac resuscitation. The Ladies' Auxiliary purchased MAX at significant cost for the hospital medical staff.

It looked foreboding. The body was a large steel table with oversized wheels. It had the appearance of an autopsy table and weighed as much as a Cadillac El Dorado. I could envision it crushing visitors against the back wall of the elevator. At least they would have the proper resuscitation equipment right at hand. An EKG machine and a ventilator were built into the table. There were numerous drawers for drugs and intravenous equipment.

The centerpiece of this monster was an automatic cardiac massager. It looked like a steel doorknob welded onto the end of a piston. Various dials and gauges regulated the depth and pressure. A patient without a heartbeat was quickly placed face up onto MAX, and the knob would supposedly compress his breastbone and squeeze the blood from his heart, instantly bringing life.

Once I awoke from a dream fearing that I was on the receiving end of this bizarre machine. A nurse or doctor was about to set the wrong pressure or distance. I even envisioned a small child or newborn mistakenly receiving treatment from MAX. Apparently I was not the only concerned physician. Several years later I found MAX languishing in the basement, next to the iron lung.

About that time, a pharmaceutical company excitedly marketed an antibiotic suppository. The bad news was that a parent was supposed to pop this medicine into the butt of their screaming, fleeing child twice a day for ten days. The good news was that it was a powerful incentive for the victim to learn how to swallow liquid medicine or pills. To be fair, I must note that five-day deodorant pads and pet rocks were in vogue that year.

Another pharmaceutical bomb in mid 1960s was the introduction of the tetracycline antibiotic drops for the treatment of childhood ear infections. My Air Force colleague told of infants in Boston returning to the emergency room several days after their initial visit with cherry liquid oozing from the ear canal. The caregiver had assumed that drops for ear infections went into the ear, not the mouth. On a more serious note there have been cases of severe liver toxicity and death in infants receiving overdoses of the fever reducer acetaminophen. The parents had inadvertently given the concentrated dropper form by teaspoon.

I remember a day when a teenager who had mowed my lawn and watched my children limped into the office.

"So what happened to your knee? There's a lot of blood in there."

"I stepped into a hole while running, Dr. Moore."

"That sounds weird." Mark was six foot eight, but the forces he was describing just didn't add up.

"Well that's what happened."

I aspirated the blood from the knee, checked for any ligament damage and immobilized Mark's knee. He went hobbling home on crutches. Two weeks later our "runner" was healed.

Ten years later we met at a party.

"Hey Dr. Moore. Remember my injured knee?"

"Yes Mark."

"I really didn't step in a hole."

"I had my doubts."

"Well, it was a quite windy spring day."

"I seem to remember that."

"I bet my brother that if I used a large beach umbrella, I could fly off the barn roof."

The parking spaces for doctors at my Air Force base were of course assigned based on rank. Those who had served our nation the longest got to park up front, and we lowly captains parked very far away. One night I drove quickly from home to the hospital to care for a child with severe croup. It seemed like a good idea to park up close in the general's spot because of this emergency. The child was very slow responding to treatment, and I was still at his bedside in the morning. A sergeant approached and tapped me on the shoulder.

"Captain. The General wants you out of his parking space. Now."

"Sergeant, I can't leave child right now."

"OK. Give me your keys."

He came back about an hour later.

"I moved your car. The gearshift was stuck and I accidentally ripped it out of the transmission. The Air Force will fix it. We did get your car out of the General's space. You're not in trouble."

When I settled down in a wintry state with three children, I remembered this episode and decided that I would purchase a different model of automobile, one that couldn't be torn apart and moved around by the hand of man.

BE A SPORT

"For when the one great scorer comes to write your name, he marks not the score but how you played the game." - Grantland Rice

To me sportsmanship means integrity, fairness, gamesmanship, honesty, principle, righteousness, sincerity and virtue. My involvement with high school athletics has been a refreshing counterpoint to the scandals which now unfortunately dominate the media coverage of the college and professional ranks.

The Maine Principal Association has established a sportsmanship code for high school students, parents, fans and coaches. For cheerleaders there is a stern warning not to disparage opponents or make noise during foul shots. Never taunt losing visiting teams with chants such as "warm up the bus" or "scoreboard". Coaches should avoid expletives and parents need to go through proper channels with complaints about school athletics.

Looking back at my own experience with high school sports in suburban New York, it seems that there were always sportsmanship issues. My ninth grade team was victimized by a fake injury play. An opposing lineman pretended to have a knee problem and fell to the ground. His quarterback declined a time out from the referees. Then, as our team wandered around waiting for their trainer to appear, the visitors quietly ambled into formation. The perpetrator quickly scrambled to his knees, the ball was hiked, and we watched in astonishment as their halfback ran around end and raced fifty yards to score.

On another occasion, our baseball team arrived for a championship away game without bats. Not the one-size-fits-all aluminum models of today, but real, old fashioned wooden bats, each with an individual weight, length, shape and feel. Just like the major leaguers, we cherished our own bats. Our opponents graciously let us borrow theirs without reservation. Somehow, like choosing the coconut-filled chocolate candy from the mixed box, we picked all the right bats and won the game.

Another time, our relay team was invited to the grand opening of an opponent's new track. I was mildly surprised when we won handily. A week later, rumor filtered back that our lane was, in fact, a few yards shorter due to a measurement error. I found my trophy for this race in my attic last year, but have no plans to return it.

Our league, the Southern Maine Athletic Association, had the usual parent-coach altercations and team drinking episodes, but over my career good sportsmanship far outweighed these bumps in the road. When Thornton Academy, the football team I looked after for forty years, played archrival Biddeford in the last regular season game each year, there was often a mixed team breakfast, and a combined band show at halftime. If a visiting football team did not bring their own physician, the other trainers and I made sure that we were available to help with any injuries or medical problems. We were never pushed to return an athlete to the field if we said he wasn't ready.

I think we were very careful never to run up the score. Having said that, the outcome of high school games could often turn in a few moments, even with large leads. You had to be careful. Once, midway through the fourth quarter, Thornton Academy was ahead by fifty points. The opposing coach bellowed across the field, berating us for scoring too many points. Looking down the long bench, I realized that *all* our players had seen action and that the cheerleaders were on deck.

Thornton Academy hosted the New England Regional Track Meet one year. The teams were often outfitted in garish fluorescent spandex. They all brought their own canopies for shade. When the javelin throwers marched across the infield, poles held high, the scene reminded me of a medieval jousting event.

The sportsmanship was outstanding. Local runners gladly gave tips on the vagaries of the starting blocks and all-weather track to the visitors from away. Participants and spectators cheered equally for their favorites and for the winners. The athletes always thanked us for care rendered in the medical tent. Both the boy's long jump and pole vault were won by short, undersized athletes. A Maine pole vaulter soared over the bar to establish a New England record as the crowd of several hundred surrounded the pit clapped in rhythmic unison. Nine months later he would set an indoor record at his college, vaulting over seventeen feet.

The week before, a female runner who would have been on a New Hampshire relay team had died in her sleep.

Her fellow athletes voted to keep their commitment to race. The public address announcer broadcast in a halting voice that the wounded relay team would run, omitting the first leg in honor of their fallen teammate. The remaining three athletes jogged the remaining three legs together. The whole team wore commemorative t-shirts. As the runners crossed the finish line, hand in hand, the only sound in the stadium was that of sobbing. At an appropriate time, everyone broke into a long standing ovation. After watching this final event, I felt that we were in good hands for the future.

FOOTBALL DAYS

My love for the game of football probably came from my father, though I inherited none of his skill. As an all-state running back, he was recruited to play for Stanford by the legendary Pop Warner. Arriving from the cornfields of Iowa, my father stood in awe of the balmy weather, palm trees, and beautiful coeds of California. Although he played well, the great depression dictated a return to his home state after two years, as there were no athletic scholarships back then. After college, my father declined an invitation to try out for the Green Bay Packers. Deciding that professional football was too difficult a way to earn a living, he took a job as a bill collector in a bad section of Detroit.

I was an average high school lineman, but my name once appeared in the New York Times. That would be the high point of my brief career. At Dartmouth I languished on the freshman B team. It was our job to run practice plays against the varsity, just as in the movie *Rudy*. As compensation the athletic director would schedule a few games for us against nearby prep schools. I remember one match where we arrived with only two spare players. Wearing torn practice uniforms, we disembarked from the bus looking like a Burt Reynolds prison team. In one of the dirtiest games I ever played in, we eked out a narrow win. As the game ended, the expensively uniformed preppies and their tweedy parents wandered around in stunned silence. Later I found out that we were heavy underdogs - but nobody told us.

By the end of the season, I was half an inch shorter,

unable to lift my arms, and sported a continual headache. I decided that my future lay not on the gridiron but rather in the chemistry lab.

When I arrived in Maine, I inherited the job of local high school physician which included patrolling the football sidelines on Saturdays. I watched for injuries, relocated shoulders, sutured lacerations and performed a host of other functions. At times it was lonely and occasionally scary. Forty years later we have a bevy of physical therapists, student managers, and orthopedic surgeons. Life is much easier. A few stories come to mind.

One afternoon a mammoth-sized tackle jogged off the field after a change of possession and asked me for some oxygen, even though his chest sounded clear. A small tank was available, used mainly to power my asthma nebulizer equipment. It was always good public relations to offer treatment to a wheezing opponent who had forgotten his puffer. I gave our air-hungry player a few puffs but he kept coming back for more.

After a while, I realized that I had become his private oxygen dealer. The gas is not cheap, and this lad's addiction to the green canister was starting to cost the program money. I decided that he could finish the season huffing on a placebo, mask firmly in place, tank shut off.

The sham treatments worked just fine - after each one he would remark "I really feel a lot better, Doc." This gentle giant went on to play football for an Ivy League school. At those prices, I hope he was given a few puffs of the real deal.

My brief and very successful stint as deputy assistant offensive coordinator took place during a playoff game. Just before halftime our running back broke off tackle and ran to midfield. My job required me to closely observe each down, looking for injured players. I noted that two defensive halfbacks on the visiting team were slow to get up. In a low voice I strongly suggested that our coach run the exact same play. He agreed, and Art L. rambled fifty yards into the end zone as time expired.

Thornton Academy football won state titles 1986 and 1988. For my contribution to each of these campaigns, I was given a varsity jacket. Wearing one instantly transports me back to my high school days. My third son David, a high school soccer player, took one of these jackets off to college. It was reported that he removed the "Dr." from the garment leaving only the family surname and the words "state football champions". He then fibbed to out-of-state classmates that he had kicked a long winning field goal in the later minutes of the final game. These stories only dribble out into the open in later years.

Road trips were always interesting. Before my arrival, the team played an occasional away game in Rumford. This northwestern mountain city has since lost population due to paper mill closures, slipped to class B, and is no longer an opponent. The players swore that the lengthy trip at times passed into Canada. Sometimes I would travel with the team. You always held your breath waiting to see if your transportation was a sleek comfortable coach or a gritty yellow school bus.

The long bus trip north to Bangor was the biggest

loser, three hours north, seventy miles to the east, almost in a different time zone. We often seemed to lose close games in Bangor. It was always sleeting. The marginally heated locker room under the concrete stands echoed like the catacombs.

The previous Thornton Academy football field was on the east side of Route 1. It was ringed by maple and oak trees, which glowed in the fall afternoons. This scene alone was worth the price of admission. At halftime, the teams would retreat across the highway to the headmaster's barn, separated by a flimsy wall. Often I stood with my mouth agape, listening to the visiting coaches spew obscenities at the top of their lungs. My most vivid memory of this beautiful old stadium is that of a thunder and lightning storm arriving as the teams began to brawl after the last play of a close game. Eventually, the school tore it down and built a new stadium across the way.

At halftime of the one hundredth game against arch-rival Biddeford, I was awarded the game ball. It was unexpected and is still treasured. The award should have been given to my family. If there are people who have served in your community for a significant time be certain to acknowledge them.

MIND OVER MATTER

My medical school introduction to psychiatry had a Freudian flavor. Our instructor even had a middle European accent. We diagrammed interactions between the id and the ego and learned about transference, sublimation and avoidance. The biochemistry of the brain was for the most part a mystery. The pharmacological tools available were few – Thorazine, phenobarbital, Librium, and a few other primitive drugs. Mental health wards were not terribly different from their famous depiction in *One Flew Over the Cuckoo's Nest*. One New York practitioner even performed outpatient frontal lobotomies with little or no sedation or consent. Early childhood events held the key to both personality and mental health disorders.

Over the next several decades, our understanding of brain microchemistry advanced rapidly. Now grandma's DNA trumped the emotional impact of her death. The formal diagnostic codes expanded exponentially – post-traumatic stress syndrome, obsessive compulsive disorder, Asberger's, and sexual addiction, to name but a few. Drug options expanded and appeared on your TV every evening- monoamine oxidase inhibitors, selective serotonin reuptake inhibitors, antipsychotics, and the list goes on.

But gradually, science is realizing that genealogy and family dynamics may interact. Through advances in imaging, we now know that early childhood emotional trauma may produce structural brain changes in areas that serve as nerve switching and relay stations, under the control of brain chemicals. Mental health diagnoses may be complex and involve both inside and outside forces.

One night during my internship I received a call from the emergency room. The doctor was puzzled.

"She's from the Caribbean, Dr. Moore. Found on the street. Don't know if she speaks English. Her labs and spinal fluid are negative. The exam and vital signs are normal but we can't wake her up. May be some sort of encephalitis."

A quick exam confirmed the findings. What to do? The answer came to me from a recent discussion with a psychiatrist at midnight supper.

Midnight supper was an almost cult-like gathering of doctors in training that took place every night in the cafeteria. Food was either free or sold at reduced fee. Nuggets of obscure medical and surgical information from unusual cases were the reason we all got together. House staff not attending these informal teaching sessions did so at their own peril. It seemed to be a ritual in every city hospital.

As a medical student, I worked as a lab technician to pay expenses. Always broke, I would eat sparingly during the day, then bargain with the cashiers at the witching hour for reduced meal prices. I became a surrogate son. While chowing down, the interns and residents would discuss difficult cases.

Back in the emergency room I implemented my supper

strategy by asking everyone to exit the examining room. They hovered at the doorframe, watching my new patient.

"Here goes nothing", I thought, and drew the hospital sheet up over this seemingly lifeless body.

"It's a shame," I said in a firm voice. "Call the priest. This patient is dead."

Nothing. I repeated the request.

Slowly the sheet moved on table. Then quickly the form sat upright, still under a sheet. It was like watching a motorized lawn display at Halloween. The diagnosis of psychiatric catatonia, a marked change in muscle activity or tone, was established. Gasps came from just beyond the door. Several of the house staff shook my hand.

But there were still two logistical matters. First I had to convince the secretary that my name should go to the bottom of the call list because I had responded and triaged this young woman. It took longer to persuade the confused psychiatric resident that the woman should be rerouted to his mental health ward. The tale of my diagnostic gamble would spread throughout the hospital. I wandered back to the ward with a smile on my face, and went back to sleep.

Several years ago, an older child came to me with constant pain over his lower sternum. The discomfort was severe and he did not respond to the usual stomach and ulcer medications. An upper gastrointestinal barium study was negative. Blood work also revealed nothing. Extensive interviews with the child uncovered no environmental or social issues. I even injected the trigger point with local anesthetic and some cortisone to no avail. He was often absent from school and his grades fell.

Exhausting all treatments the child went to live with his grandmother in a different school district. Within days the pain went away. I suspected anxiety caused by bullying but was never able to prove it.

On another occasion the nurse on the pediatric ward phoned me urgently.

"Your toddler with croup is getting worse. You need to come over now."

Leaving a busy office, I arrived at the crib with some apprehension. A gathering of nurses, respiratory technicians, and assorted onlookers stood watching a blue struggling infant. I reviewed his course to date. "Admitted three days ago with croup. Gradually weaned from oxygen and IVs." On morning rounds he appeared to be improving. Now he was frantic with poor color and wheezing.

I had an idea. "Mrs. F," I urged softly, "Please give the baby a bottle".

"I can't do that, Dr. Moore. He's in too much distress."

"Please do it."

We all held our breath. The struggling infant snatched the bottle instantly. After a minute of gulping his first food in three days, all of his symptoms vanished. I then headed down to the cafeteria for a quick bite of lunch myself.

From the suddenly mute eight-year-old with a sexually abusive father, to my severe stuttering in grade school when my father was away at war, the mind-body connection is powerful. I have learned the hard way to pursue both paths in parallel when confronted with bizarre or unusual symptoms.

SARAH

Sarah was a regular patient. Her mother brought her in for a fifteen-month well baby check, but unfortunately some "well babies" aren't. Sarah's day care staff was concerned about her weight loss, diarrhea and possible developmental regression. At times she would sit alone while sucking on her fingers. The last symptom was very disturbing. During my residency, I had contact with a number of children with progressive neurological disease. The possible diagnoses would fill several textbook pages. I envisioned seizures and feeding tubes.

I have a slide picture of a pot-bellied, stick legged Sarah being supported by her father. She did not appear well. I told Sarah's parents that I needed to send her to Boston for some tests that we could not provide. They quickly agreed.

My concern was Rett Syndrome, a progressive neurological disease found only in females. I sent Sarah to a well-regarded development center. The specialists ruled out Rett Syndrome but offered no alternative diagnosis. The family returned to Maine.

"She's getting worse, Dr. Moore. We need a diagnosis."

Sarah was now appearing quite pale. Her mild anemia had become significant. But suddenly I had another piece of the puzzle that the Boston doctors lacked. Developmental regression plus anemia sent us down a completely different road. Dietary iron deficiency in a child receiving balanced meals would be unlikely without blood loss or the poor absorption of food. Tests

141

showed no blood loss. There is a long list of diseases that prevent food from being absorbed from the small bowel. Moreover, the brain is dependent on vitamins and minerals to function well. Where to start?

A normal sweat chloride test ruled out cystic fibrosis, a common cause of childhood malnutrition. However, her levels of iron, zinc and vitamin A were low. The best test for poor absorption at that time was a blood xylose test. Xylose is a sugar that only occurs in trace amounts in fruits and vegetables. So it shouldn't be in your body, unless you chew sugarless gum. Sarah was given a xylose drink and we measured her xylose blood level an hour later. It was low. We now had evidence of malabsorption.

Celiac disease is caused by an adverse reaction to gluten, the sticky component of wheat. You remember from high school science, unless you were dozing, that the villae in the small bowel look like tiny fingers hanging down from the bowel wall. They have a large surface area, the size of a tennis court that makes them ideal for absorbing food. Wheat gluten causes inflammation of this wall, just like dust or ragweed inflames the air sacs in the lungs. The damage is complicated to explain, but the injured villae become stunted and flat. They just don't work as they should.

Babies usually aren't fed cereal until a few months of age, so celiac disease takes time to develop. Three other children in my practice who suffered from this disease were diagnosed later in childhood with suboptimal growth or chronic diarrhea.

Small bowel biopsy is still the gold standard for diagnosing celiac disease. In Sarah's time, believe it or not, a child ingested a capsule on a string and a guillotine mechanism chopped off a bit of the bowel wall. The next advance was endoscopy where the doctor could insert a flexible telescope into the patient and actually look at the bowel. Today, the surface of the bowel can be seen by a tiny camera in a capsule that is swallowed. I sent Sarah back to Boston to see a friend of mine, Dr. Richard Grand. He confirmed the diagnosis with a biopsy. A gluten-free diet for Sarah produced a dramatic weight gain and reversed her regression. A photo from several months later shows a smiling Sarah, ten pounds heavier, sitting on my infant scale.

Today, there are new blood tests that can screen for celiac disease. Physicians now realize that the majority of new patients with this malady present with strange and sneaky symptoms at an older age. If the disease is not on a pediatrician's radar screen, it may escape detection for years. A study from France showed that if celiac disease is missed in childhood it may lead to short stature, cancer, early osteoporosis, infertility, acute liver failure, and a host of other maladies. The disease is now thought to strike almost one in a hundred in the general US population, making it anything but rare; those with a celiac relative, diabetes or Down syndrome are at even greater risk. You may have a friend or relative with unexplained weight loss, osteoporosis at a young age, chronic bowel problems, undiagnosed anemia, or just chronic fatigue. Consider this diagnosis.

Sarah's family was able to purchase gluten-free foods from a local natural food store. Today, these special items are widely distributed in almost every grocery chain. Researchers are experimenting with new aids and treatments for celiac disease, such as gluten-free wheat and drugs to prevent bowel wall inflammation. Sarah is now in college; slim and trim. She has a personal early warning system - when she strays from her diet, cramping quickly follows. It is encouraging for her and others to know that this disease can be conquered simply by eating the correct foods.

REAR ENDED

The pediatric emergency room infant examining area in one city hospital was perhaps twenty feet square. Circling the periphery was a countertop at a height of three feet. Twenty-four hours per day, seven days a week the ledge was filled with screaming infants. The noise was earsplitting. As internist in training, I often walked past this door on the way to the adult emergency room. It was a different planet inside those walls. One day a fellow intern mumbled to me as we passed.

"Wow. I don't know how a doctor could do pediatrics for a lifetime. Listening to that racket and treating diaper rashes all day long. That doesn't seem very fulfilling."

At that time, having sparse training and little interest in the care of children, I agreed.

It turned out that pediatrics was much more complicated and rewarding than an uninterrupted sequence of diaper rash. As the muffler shop might advertise, we also do pneumonia, newborns, diabetes, trauma, lacerations, mental health and a host of other maladies. Having said that, parents often consider the smallest blemish as a stark indicator of bad parenting.

"Hey Dr. Moore, get down to the office. You have three patients waiting," urged nurse Dotty.

"Dotty. It snowed two feet last night. How did anybody drive in?"

"Never mind. Just get here. Soon."

My VW skidded down a barely plowed Route 1 into Saco. At the office Dotty ushered me towards the sickest infant.

"I came all the way down from Limington in the truck. Went off the road once. I can't stop the bleeding", blurted the frantic father. With that, he flipped back the quilt. I envisioned a blood transfusion and a race to the medical center.

He quickly opened the diaper and with a flourish exposed a moderately inflamed diaper rash. There was some slight bleeding around the edges.

"Glad that I got through the storm", father confessed. I let out a huge sigh and reassured him that we could help his son.

The evolution of diapers is far more interesting than the rashes they hide or heal. One can only imagine the nasty butt rashes of ancient times caused by diapers of grass or moss held in place by large leaves or animal skins. In the last century advances in bacteriology and absorbent materials yielded great improvements in both cloth and disposable diapers. Super-absorbent polymers, wetness indicators, and glow in the dark tabs are some of the technologies that you can find in a diaper but not in my Hyundai. There has been a modest resurgence of cloth diapers for financial and environmental reasons. Mothers have shown me new and ingenious cloth diaper systems practically every week.

My phone rang at home after midnight. "Dr. Moore", a frantic mother stammered. "My son has some terrible tropical disease. I went to change his diaper and it was full of this gooey stuff. Looks like worms. I don't know where they came from. Haven't been out of New England in years. It looks awful."

This description prompted my favorite scheme for buying time until the morning.

"This is not serious. But, you have a very important job to do. Listen carefully. Please save this diaper and any others like it and make an appointment to see me tomorrow. OK?"

Having parents save the body fluids of their sick child makes them feel like you are seriously focused on the problem. It's like boiling water for the farm kitchen appendectomy.

"Yes, doctor", the relieved mother sighed.

In the next morning's light, this sandy tapioca gel was unlike anything seen before. Under the microscope it looked like sandy tapioca. A nurse stuck her head into the exam room and suggested that the goop might be absorbent material from inside the diaper. With the nurse assisting, we carefully dissected the diaper with scissors, and voila – the same unpleasant gel was inside. My past training had not prepared me for this newly marketed SAP (super absorbent polymer). Pediatric journal articles soon alerted physicians to this mystery. One company investigated the concept of a flushable disposable diaper. A pediatrician then concluded that the only possible benefit from this new item would be that we could all walk to Europe in five years. Two companies claimed they had developed a biodegradable diaper in the early 1980s, but the F.T.C. pulled the naughty napkins from the shelves, citing insufficient evidence that they would decompose in a reasonable time.

Cloth diapers also have a few drawbacks. I refer you to *The Prevention and Cure of Diseases,* written by William Buchan in 1783. "Pins have been found sticking above half an inch into the body of a child, after it had died of convulsion-fits, which in all probability, preceded from the cause." I have witnessed pin pain several times, though no child has ever died.

In 1946, housewife Marion Donovan invented the "Boater", a plastic waterproof diaper covering. The wrap was fastened by plastic snaps, sounding the death knell for the *safety* pin.

Finally, a young infant who was brought to the office because of a bruise over the top of his head. The large purple spot looked nasty. A serious blood disease or even child abuse came to mind. The remainder of the exam was unremarkable. As a stalling tactic we asked the mother to go home have some lunch while our staff mulled the next step.

The mother called back a few days later.

"It's the diapers," she stated emphatically.

"How is that?" I puzzled.

"I noticed that Sam's head was rubbing up against the purple dye on the side of the diaper box. You know, the one with big baby's head. Some dye came off on my finger when I wiped it on the box. I washed the purple off his scalp with rubbing alcohol. He's cured."

Resisting the temptation to fib that Sam's doctor was just considering the same answer, congratulations were given to Sam's mother on her keen diagnostic skills. One of my cardinal rules about unusual skin problems had been ignored. Before you start the thousand-dollar work-up on a child with a localized rash, see if it will disappear with a swipe of an alcohol pad.

A ROYAL PAIN

"Hey, Doc, your patient didn't do so well while you were on vacation."

The ward nurse was filling me in on James, who had undergone an appendectomy while I was away. Afterwards he was in severe pain. Narcotics didn't help and he became quite loud and combative. He was put in restraints. The nurses had never seen anything like it. Even stranger than his symptoms was the fact that his appendix was normal and was not the cause of his torment.

I lost track of James for a while. A few years later, at age nineteen, he was readmitted for similar symptoms. The list of possible diagnoses for recurrent severe abdominal pain include abdominal migraine, lead poisoning, gall bladder problems, twisted bowel, and finally, porphyria.

Porphyria is a disease of heme production. Heme is a critical building block in many body systems, especially hemoglobin which is the red material inside blood cells. Porphyria is derived from the Greek word for purple. Patients with porphyria lack various enzymes along the eight-step assembly line which culminates in the formation of hemoglobin. Because of the missing enzymes, stalled chemicals become toxic as they increase in amount. The location of the blockage dictates the symptoms. Leaking out into the body they injure different tissues and sometimes color the urine purple. There are eight types of porphyria and many subtypes. One form of porphyria produces blistering skin and sensitivity to sunlight.

Porphyria has figured in European history and literature. King George III is perhaps the most famous case. Various medical historians have attributed his madness to porphyria, but others disagree. Retrospective diagnoses are always difficult, and to further complicate things, many treatments of this era contained toxic heavy metals such as arsenic, antimony and lead. Syphilis was another ever-present danger to the human brain. But the great-great-great-grandson of King George III, Prince William of Gloucester, was definitely diagnosed with porphyria by several experts in the 1970s. DNA testing on the bones of Charlotte of Prussia, another descendant, strongly suggested porphyria. The blistering caused by porphyria may explain some of the folklore concerning werewolves, as scarring from sun sensitivity can result in new tissue with coarse hairs.

Though usually hereditary, porphyria can be induced by liver damage from chronic alcoholism. I can still remember being a medical student and placing urine bottles onto the sunny city hospital ward window sills and hoping for a purple hue that would earn me brownie points from the chief resident. It never happened for me but it did for a colleague. In the 1950s an agricultural accident in Turkey released hexachlorobenzine, a wheat fungicide, into the bread supply. This chemical caused porphyria of the liver and there were hundreds of deaths.

I did not fully evaluate James before he vanished again. His urine did contain elevated levels of a compound in the heme assembly line, as well as low amounts of one critical enzyme. Though some pieces of the puzzle were missing, I told James that he had some form of porphyria. We made him aware of the drugs that were known to trigger episodes of this disease.

Treatment of the most commons types of porphyria includes avoiding stress, sunlight, infection and certain medications. Remedies for acute episodes include narcotics for pain, intravenous fluids, and the actual infusion of heme. A stem cell transplant is the last resort, but this procedure is not without peril. Gene therapy holds promise for the future - fox squirrels are wired for skin porphyria but don't become ill, and the chlorophyll in plants is made in a fashion similar to heme.

MISUNDERSTANDINGS

The ability to communicate clearly is one of the most important skills a physician can possess. Fortunately, most of my misunderstandings have been minor and even comic.

At a kindergarten physical I was doing an examination of the private parts right after the eye test. Suddenly the mother blurted out "He still calls that a tiger!"

Never at a loss for words, I mumbled on about a recent list of odd and unusual names used by English children to identify their genitalia. The whole vocabulary had been published in a respected British pediatric medical journal.

After a short while, mother waved her hands and almost shouted "No, no – I mean that picture on the eye chart!"

Eye charts often cause confusion. Preschool children are asked to identify objects rather than letters, but most children today have never seen the cradle phone depicted on my out-of-date chart. Other figures evoke a wide variety of answers, like a kindergarten Rorschach test. Older patients are given a plastic paddle, looking like a giant lollipop, to cover the unexamined eye. I don't want to say that they are prone to cheating, but the examinees do like to peek around the edge of the paddle, necessitating the pirate patch. Problems often arise when the child is then asked to cover the other eye. "Hey Doctor Moore, now I can't see anything."

Having a patient get ready for an examination was a

common point of failure. On occasion an adolescent would enter from the adjoining bathroom with the mandatory white gown tied tightly over street clothes. Sexually active teens would arrive wearing six layers, feigning modesty, when level three was removed, protesting that "I just don't feel comfortable." On the flip side, I witnessed many buck-naked flower children saunter through the same door and hop up onto the exam table. Another time I was discussing the onset of womanhood to a young teen. I then too rapidly switched to bicycle safety - "make sure you wear a helmet!" The puzzled patient then asked, in all seriousness, "Dr. Moore, why do you want me to wear a bike helmet during my period?"

Misunderstandings may involve the authorities. Many years ago a foreboding envelope from New York State Police arrived amid the usual junk mail. It had seals, flags, and bold lettering. What had I done now? How much trouble was I in? I searched my mind for a link. Then a recent event slowly came to mind.

I had been driving on a divided parkway in that state, when a motorcyclist ahead of me skidded off the road and down an embankment. I pulled over and sprinted down to the driver. He had obviously broken his leg, but that seemed to be the extent of the damage. As usual, I had my football bag in the trunk. I was able to splint the fracture and get the frightened biker wrapped up in a blanket. A few minutes later the state police arrived. They determined the location of the nearest hospital and radioed for an ambulance. The victim remained alert and only complained of leg pain. His pulse remained strong and slow.

156

I helped load him into the ambulance. The trooper asked me for a report of the accident as well as my name and address. The event delayed me for an hour but I was glad to help. It didn't seem like a big deal. I had heard stories from several other Maine doctors about helping accident victims on the road.

I looked at the official envelope again. Did I break some law? Was I being sued?

I slowly opened the envelope, then gave of a sigh of relief. The police were just thanking me for stopping. Then they added."We doubt the physicians in our state would have stopped."

A child had been brought from Indiana to the Cincinnati Children's Hospital because she was febrile and poorly responsive. She had contracted measles several months prior but had recovered well. Her neck was stiff and pus drained from her ear canals. Her spinal fluid was cloudy but no bacteria were seen under the microscope nor grown from the culture. Her tuberculosis skin test was negative. This case did not add up.

I asked the intern about the chest x-ray.

"Negative!" he answered crisply.

The next day we were no further ahead. I asked the intern for the x-ray report.

"Not ready yet", he volunteered.

"How about just bringing me the x-ray then?"

Thirty minutes later he returned. "Ahh . . . the films were never taken," he confessed.

Lesson learned. Never assume that just because you ordered lab and x-ray studied that they were actually done.

The chest x-ray was then actually taken and it revealed extensive tuberculosis. The child recovered. We had ignored a simple adage handed down by old-time practitioners - "Tuberculosis follows measles like a shadow."

One day I was removing a foreign body from the cornea of an older child. We had the exam room lights off and I was using a head lamp. The youngster was a bit apprehensive and mother replied that she would hold his hold his hand. The procedure went well, but when the lights went on, it seemed that the mother was holding MY hand. This became a running joke in the office for years.

Sometimes I misunderstood the reaction of a parent. It was a summer Saturday afternoon. A family was visiting from Connecticut and I had just given the infant an antibiotic injection. As per my usual routine, I scooped her up over my shoulder while rubbing her back and singing gently.

After a while I glanced at the parents. They were frowning and looking right through me. Had I explained the need for this shot? Was there blood spurting from the puncture? Did my quick stick indicate a primitive style of medicine?

"Is everything OK?" I asked.

The parents whispered to each other.

"We've never seen a doctor pick up a baby before," they confessed.

I started to suggest that they change doctors when they arrived home, but offered this instead.

"Well, it's an old Maine custom. The nurses taught me."

It was well into the evening of a long day at the office. I was examining the infant of a family belonging to another pediatrician. The mother looked a bit plump and was wearing what looked like a maternity dress. I was making polite conversation with a tired mind.

"When is your due date?"

"I'm not pregnant, Dr. Moore."

My rapid recovery was one of the high points of my career. "No, no", I chuckled falsely. "I was talking about your toddler. Was he a preemie? I need to know for his antibiotic choice."

"Oh. I thought you were talking about me."

" No, no", I laughed nervously.

Two ironclad rules for any new doctors- never ask a woman her due date unless you are sure that she is pregnant, and *never, ever* walk through the emergency room on your day off.

FORMULA FOR SUCCESS

Prior to modern baby formula, it was observed that breast fed infants had a greater survival rate than those who were not. During the middle ages, babies had the advantage of an extended family with many wet nurses. When this network began to fracture, milk feeding flourished. Various glass and ceramic feeders appeared. The Windship feeder was a hollow glass breast to be concealed under the clothing – mimicking the human real deal. Early rubber nipples were difficult to clean and bacteria could hide in the cracks. The Pratt nipple was outlawed in 1897 in Buffalo, New York as the "murder nipple".

In the late 19th century epidemic diarrhea led to countless deaths in urban children. The culprit may have been pathogenic E. coli but the medical community lacked today's microbiological tools to make this diagnosis. Milk stations were established to provide daily "clean" milk to city families. This goal proved elusive, however, because of the difficulty of daily purchase and lack of refrigeration. Boiled milk had problems with taste and texture but pasteurization provided an acceptable product. These advances led to evaporated milk, which does not need refrigeration until it is opened. Add a bit of corn syrup and water and you have instant infant formula.

Harvard's first professor of pediatrics, Dr. Thomas Rotch, felt the feeding of babies was so important that the details should not be left to mothers or manufacturers. He devised calculations for the protein content of each bottle for each individual infant, hence the term formula. His elaborate milk equations look like a calculus exam- eventually too complex for the general public. Soon Vitamins C and D were added to prevent scurvy and rickets. Minerals came next. However, locals have related that in past decades some families preferred plain iron-free evaporated milk formula because it gave their babies such a nice complexion- which was actually due to profound anemia. Despite all these advances, as a medical student in the 1960s I was still eyeballing mixtures of evaporated milk, sugar and water.

The percentage of American infants initially breast fed dipped to twenty per cent in the 1950s. Through the efforts of many groups, such as La Leche, the American Academy of Pediatrics, and hospital based lactation consultants, this rate has risen to seventy percent at time of discharge. The rate falls off steadily over the next six months and more support for nursing mothers is needed. The lactation nurses at our local hospital have established an excellent program to foster breast feeding– with prenatal seminars, lessons in the hospital, and follow-up visits.

The advantages of breast milk are legion. Every year there are additional medical articles touting some new benefit of breast milk - slightly higher IQ, less colic, and decreased allergies, eczema, diarrheal illness, ear infections...the list goes on.

When I arrived in Maine, formula was crude by today's standards. There was no super-refined formula for infants with severe allergies. The soy formula tasted like an alfalfa-based wallpaper paste mix. It produced watery stool with an indescribable odor. Gerber had formula with beef and lamb for the fussier babies. These bizarre products were occasionally helpful, as was local goat milk. Steadily, through research, the protein in special formula was chemically broken down into ever smaller pieces, rendering it less allergic.

Back then the formula for premature infants often did not produce adequate growth- so we made our own. Starting with dextromaltose sugar, we then added liquid fat, protein powder, vitamins and minerals. The premature infants seemed to thrive.

Breast will always be best, but varieties of excellent substitutes are available if needed. Today, a veritable warehouse of vitamins and minerals has been blended into standard formula. Omega fatty acids, now added to mimic breast milk, will give your child the sight of a hawk and a mind ready for Harvard. Infant nutrition is second only to immunization as a pediatric success story.

DOORKNOB DILEMMAS

This is not a chapter about interior decorating, but rather a topic so vexing that it was discussed at a recent conference for medical students and residents. The question is what to do next when Mrs. Jones, her hand on the doorknob as she leaves after her child's visit, says "Oh doctor! I forgot to ask you to check Johnny for ADHD, rectal bleeding, and school failure."

If you don't address the plea, you will be seen as uncaring and money grabbing. If you respond, the waiting room will back up into the parking lot.

A friend claims her pediatrician was the doorknob problem. According to her, this doctor would stand half in the doorway, ready to race to the next exam room, while asking if she had any questions.

Sometimes the doorknob pause may be a lifesaver. One mother scheduled a visit for diaper rash. For twenty minutes we discussed creams, diets, different diapers, and a host of other topics. The mother seemed satisfied but on the way out asked me to take a quick peek at her eight-year-old daughter, who had been quietly reading in the corner. She pulled her daughter up close to me.

"I have been getting her shoulder manipulated for several months, but her arm still doesn't work too well."

To my amazement, the child produced a limp right arm with her fingers locked into a claw. A quick exam suggested a neurological problem at the neck, perhaps some sort of mass. The final diagnosis was a benign tumor pressing on the spinal cord. It was successfully removed with good return of arm and hand function.

On another occasion, on her way out the door, a mother asked "Dr. Moore, I'm about to set up my child with an eye exercise program to cure his learning disability. Is that a good idea?"

"No. Please don't do that."

"O.K."

Sometimes it is the nurse's hand on the doorknob. I had just finished examining an infant with abdominal pain. He was on his way home with a pre-printed gastroenteritis instruction sheet when nurse Judy barred the door.

"How do you know this child doesn't have an intussusception?"

Intussusception is a condition where a section of bowel slides inside of an adjacent section and gets caught. The trapped bowel can lose blood, perforate, and cause death.

Never ignore comments from your nurse. An emergency barium enema confirmed the diagnosis. By holding the barium bag three feet above the infant we were able to pop the bowel back into place and avoid surgery. The toddler did well.

Another time a two year old had the same symptoms

but some vomiting and mild fever. I was about to send him home with the usual diet of small sips of clear fluids. His abdomen was fairly soft and free of pain when I felt it. My hand was on the knob. Suddenly mother spoke in a worried tone.

"Is my child going to be OK?"

I never get quite used to that question. It was mid-afternoon on a Friday. In a few hours, despite excellent coverage by other pediatricians, the toddler was about to be swallowed up by the weekend. I would worry about him for two days. I asked my lab tech Nancy to do a white blood count and we could all go home smiling.

But the white blood cell count was four times normal, a clear indicator that his appendix had ruptured. We were able to find the pediatric surgeon at the medical center before the weekend descended. This mother's intuition may have saved her child.

Another time my hand was on the doorknob when I was giving last minute instruction to a mother. I had just diagnosed her young infant with a urinary infection. The child's temperature was 105 degrees. Suddenly her mom began to stammer with a glazed look to her eyes. "Please pay attention, Mrs. X.," I ordered somewhat sternly. "If you listen carefully your baby will do just fine." Mrs. X remained mute and finally pointed a shaking finger in the direction of her now-seizing infant on the exam table. The baby did well. To her credit, mother continued to bring this child and, eventually, her grandchildren back to see me.

GO PEE IN THIS CUP

These five words are uttered by nurses and doctors around the world thousands of times a day. The instructions are simple, but in my career there were countless misunderstandings.

A father once came down the hall with his child – both with urine cups in hand. He was the one who signed his child in, so he felt compelled to follow the perhaps unclear instructions on the sheet – please go and bring back a full urine cup.

Some children brought back several cups, carrying them with the grace and skill of Oktoberfest waitresses. I never bothered to find out whether they thought I was testing them for bladder volume.

One teen couldn't pee and was asked to drink fluids. He took a short ride down the street and came back with his urine in a McDonald's cup.

Several patients returned with a "urine" sample that had obviously come out of our bathroom taps. I resisted the temptation to stick my finger in, lick it, and proclaim a clean bill of health.

Still other children and teens were initially unable to pee. They were then asked to drink water but were indignant when they were given only ONE standard Dixie cup to complete both requests - most pediatricians are tight with supplies.

Several patients urinated in the cup, and proceed to

dump the contents into toilet. When they brought the empty cup back to the nurse I always made sure they were given credit for a correct, if perhaps too literal, interpretation of their task.

On my very first weekend in Maine I had finished morning office hours and wandered out to the lobby to lock the front door. An elderly gentleman was sitting alone.

"Is your grandchild in the bathroom?" I inquired.

"Hell no," he boomed in a friendly voice. "I saw your name on the building. Sign said M.D. Hurts when I pass my water. On vacation. Just me."

I started to explain the age parameters of pediatrics and the importance of specialization. This senior citizen wasn't listening and seemed uncomfortable.

He was correct. I am a doctor and I had done an internship in internal medicine before the Air Force converted me into a pediatrician. I remembered a paragraph from the modern Hippocratic Oath." I will apply for the benefit of the sick; all measures required and avoid the twin traps of overtreatment and therapeutic nihilism." If sent to the emergency room he would wait for several hours. There were no full time hospital-based doctors in the emergency room. The on-call physician would have to grumble in from home to see him.

A urine sample showed evidence of a bladder infection. I may even have done a prostate exam. My new friend left with some antibiotic samples and note for his own doctor on my prescription pad, with "infants and children" delicately crossed off the letterhead.

"How much do I owe you?"

"No charge. Kept you waiting too long", I apologized.

"You Maine folks are very kind", he smiled.

FREEDOM OF CHOICE

There is no doubt that modern Americans are besieged by too many choices. In my father's time Henry Ford offered the Models T and A in any color the customer wished - as long as it was black. As a first grader in the dairy state of Wisconsin six decades ago, my cone flavors were limited to the basic three - single scoop five cents, double was seven. Now through the magic of Madison Avenue, TV, the web, and Ben and Jerry, the choices are infinite. The same holds true for breakfast cereals, hair styles, coffee flavors, and car colors.

Even while typing this chapter, there are three remote controls within reach - television, propane stove, and a mouse for the computer. Until my second cup of coffee I will often attempt to cut and paste with the TV zapper or heat up the room via the mouse. It doesn't bother me anymore, as friends relate similar choice challenges.

I still have problems navigating fast food menu boards. I don't use these rapid restaurants frequently – usually when on the road or when the elements have yet again knocked out the power at home. I stand there with glazed eyes, trying to match the meaningless descriptions with the correct pictograph. Only the counterperson noting that "Hey, Dr. Moore for fifty cents more you can add six hundred calories", stirs me from this reverie.

To ease the pain of a blood draw or suturing, the children in our practice would be offered a treasure box, brimming with toys, games, and trinkets. The child may be having a bad day or possess an established attention problem. Twenty minutes later the youngster could be found sitting cross legged in the hallway – still sorting through the dozens of choices. Attempts to expedite this process would immediately undo all of the prior goodwill.

A surprising number of parents are unable to successfully navigate the minefield of modern baby names. The first sentence of our Canadian book of children's names gently warns, "please don't get cute with your newborn's name, they will wear it throughout their life." Sometimes parents have not fully discussed the spelling of the name prior to delivery- evoking an audible gasp from the attending nurse as she begins to fill out the birth certificate. Later in our office my receptionist often encounters the following- " Her name is Kaleleigh. You should know how to spell that."

One mother was so enamored with the name of her first child that she gave her second the same name. I feared one child would be immunized twice and the other not at all. Moreover, one could predict that the public school system would not be pleased. We prevailed upon this mother to initiate a formal name change. Another mother has my gratitude for naming her girls with comforting names from my childhood – Barbara and Susan. My pediatrician son and I had a running contest to see who could treat the child with the most unusual name. Both privacy and judgment issues have lead to the deletion of actual names from this sentence.

Finally, there has been a trend for more expressive adjectives to describe ill children. In the past a child was well, sick, very sick or call the ambulance. Now, an expanded vocabulary has evolved.

"The day care says Brahgman is *lethargic*."

"Cyndee seems to have *malaise*."

There are too many choices. Take the letter "L" for example. To date we have lazy, listless, lethargic, limp, languid, lackadaisical, languorous and maybe more to describe a sick child. Perhaps we pediatricians should just talk to the child directly on the phone. Then WE could interpret the meaning of YUCKIE.

LAW AND ORDER

Shortly after my arrival in Maine, I received a call from the Old Orchard Police. One of my teen patients had been arrested for drunk driving. In those days, the defendant could select the person to draw his blood for alcohol level. My loyal patient decided, at midnight, that his pediatrician would be an excellent choice. For reasons that escape me today, I went. The desk sergeant watched in amazement as I sleepily shuffled through the door. My charge was in surprisingly good spirits.

"Thanks for coming down, Dr. Moore. My blood level will be OK. I think it will be a better test if you take the blood. I've found a vein right here. The needle will fit right in. Man, I'm hungry. Did you bring any food?"

The odor of alcohol wafted through the stuffy summer jailhouse air.

"Sam. Do you really, really want me to do this?"

"Yes I do. We'll show 'em."

Actually Sam was in a lose-lose game. Failure to submit to testing is an automatic guilty plea. My only hope was to prolong the conversation another three to four hours. The officer quickly put a stop to that plan. I never received Sam's level but he did make the local safety column.

Sometimes I have played the role of wannabe cop. Our emergency room had a red phone connected directly to the police station. You just had to pick up the receiver

177

for action. No need to dial or speak.

Late one summer evening I was leaving the hospital through the emergency room, which is never a good idea. A drunken patient was threatening several nurses. Never breaking stride, I pointed to the phone, waited for a nurse to give me a thumbs up sign, picked up the receiver, and walked out the door. By the time I reached my car in the parking lot I counted three police cars, lights flashing, and sirens off, heading down the hospital access road.

Another winter night, in the same emergency room, I was examining a cute blond five year old with an earache. She was dressed in her teddy bear nightgown. Just outside the door, I suddenly was aware of a small inebriated patient. The man was sitting on a metal chair, shouting nasty invectives while simultaneously complaining about the French and the poor service at this particular hospital.

My young patient appeared puzzled while I winced. The drunk was unattended as there were several emergencies in progress. If there were any security guards at that time, they were elsewhere. The language had to cease. Now.

I gently lifted the man off the chair by his sweater, pinned his shoulders against the wall, and looked into his soul. A quick explanation of our red phone ensued. He was also shown a large snow bank just outside the glass doors. Despite his blood alcohol level, the complainer seemed to grasp the consequences of any further speech. Back onto his chair he went. Several minutes later, I overheard a nurse comment on the patient's sudden attitude adjustment.

I have only been inside a police car twice. Once I was illegally transported to the hospital with a bout of appendicitis. The detective was a friend and I didn't want to tie up an ambulance. The other trip involved a premature birth. The cops found me at a local football game and whisked me away – full siren with Christopher in the back seat. Much of the time we were in the opposite lane. My son sat in stunned silence. The baby did well.

If you want the contents of your car to stay private, follow the traffic rules. One snowy night, as I was about to leave the office, a car skidded around the corner and came to rest on top of a snow bank across the street. It appeared that no one was injured, but the teens were yelling about quickly getting all four wheels back on the ground. I dialed the police and told them what was happening.

"You might ask the kids to pop the trunk. They seem to be in a big hurry to leave."

"Thanks, Doc."

My hunch proved correct. The cop arrived, the trunk went up, and two more squad cars arrived shortly.

Some years later my secretary was given a noontime ticket for driving without lights when her wipers were on – a violation in Maine. My first parent that afternoon was a Portland police officer. I asked him how often he wrote a similar ticket. Rarely, he confessed. However, the last time he did, the central computer didn't like the license and a few kilograms of narcotics were discovered.

I was always nervous in the courtroom. Despite testifying a number of times, the sound of the witness box as it banged shut followed by the taking of the oath were always unsettling. Sometimes the script did not go as planned.

The defendant had been thrown through the window of a dry cleaning store during a wedding reception. I had been called to the emergency room at 3 AM to suture his facial lacerations. At the time I noted that he had no alcohol on his breath and entered that fact in his chart. The trial centered on assault charges. During my pre-trial discussion with his lawyer, the defendant's odorless breath seemed important. The counselor and I agreed that sobriety would be relevant. On the stand, however, this fact was never addressed. I was hesitant to bring up the subject *de novo* for fear of mistrial.

Another time I was subpoenaed for similar assault trial. A teenage girl had accepted a ride to school from a neighbor. She alleged that he then forced her into the woods and delivered several hammer blows to her head. I had repaired the lacerations. But there were two problems with the story. There was no evidence of sexual assault and there were numerous comments from friends that the defendant was incapable of such an attack.

I testified for the prosecution on day two. Both lawyers were focused. We discussed everything from the age and appearance of the wounds to the mental state of the victim. Seemingly, bizarre questions were asked.

Because of my call schedule, I was unable to attend the first day of the trial and I had no frame of reference. That night when Wendy asked, I thought that the neighbor was guilty as charged. However, the next day, just as the trial went to jury, the young woman confessed through sobs that her stepfather was the assailant. He had threatened her with death if she related the true story.

BE PREPARED

Robert Bayden-Powell, the founder of organized youth scouting, took this motto for his boy's group. The full quotation goes on to explain that we all need to "be prepared in mind by having thought out beforehand an accident or situation that might occur – so that we can know the right thing to do at the right time and are willing to do it". As a physician it is second nature for me to be prepared for emergencies.

One August, when Christopher was ten, we took the eight-mile hike to Russell Pond in Baxter State Park. We fished on the evening of our arrival and caught our limit of trout in thirty minutes. Ducks landed in formation, skidding along the glassy surface. At the far edge of the pond a dripping moose foraged for his dinner. The sunset was a brilliant magenta and pink. I didn't even try to capture this scene on film.

After supper, we conversed with a honeymooning couple from Indiana. These friendly Midwest hikers had all the expensive gear they needed, but lacked experience in the woods. Dehydrated food had been their staple for a long week, and the menu had been taking its toll. We may have saved a marriage by inviting the pair over for a trout and blueberry breakfast the next day.

Somebody ambled by and said the ranger was looking for me. I attempt to keep a low profile on vacation, but perhaps there was some mention of my vocation on the registration card.

"Thanks doc," boomed the warden with a smile. "I hope you're not a psychiatrist."

A fisherman had embedded a lure into his upper eyelid. The nearest emergency room was thirty miles away in Millinocket. This city in the woods was however, a float plane trip from Russell Pond or an eight mile hike through swamp to the parking lot. Neither was highly recommended. The thought of the hook working its way through the lid and gouging the eyeball was not comforting.

There are several ways of removing fish hooks. My hook removal training began many years ago during bluefish season in Saco Bay. The local children were unaware of the danger presented by this species, which can bite your finger off. A bluefish needs to be beaten senseless with a heavy stick as soon as you get it within swinging distance. Severe bites were rare, but many children ended up in my office with deep hook wounds after attempting to manually retrieve a lure from the mouth of a bluefish. "No, I cannot get your lure out with the hooks intact. Yes, I will weigh your prize fish on my baby scale."

The ranger had small mosquito forceps used for tying flies which I used to hold the hook. We had good illumination from a Coleman lantern. The ranger produced some iodine. In those days, before box-cutter terrorism, I used to carry an #11 Bard-Parker scalpel blade in my wallet. This blade has a very fine tip, especially useful for removing splinters and tics. The antibiotic eye ointment that I always include in my backpacking first aid kit completed the gear for this makeshift operating room.

The procedure went smoothly, but please do not try eyelid hook removal at home. Our fisherman understood the consequences of any quick movements and I was able to gingerly enlarge the entry wound by one millimeter with the tip of scalpel - just enough to free the barb and pull the hook back out. His cornea had not been injured.

With advice to place the ointment over the wound every two hours and to check in with his doctor at home regarding tetanus, the patient departed the next morning.

Though my children claim that duct tape and super glue can fix any problem and even bring about world peace, I am partial to pink tape. This amazing product may have entered our hospital inadvertently, perhaps in the Isolette of a baby returning by ambulance from a Boston hospital. This very sticky half inch tape is an essential tool for caring for sick babies and infants. It can hold breathing tubes in place, secure IV needles, and build a scaffold for holding umbilical catheters in place. It seems that every few months we would find another medical use for this low tech product. This week I found a ten year old roll in my toolbox. It still had awesome adhesion.

The 8 x 10 blue tarp has been a Maine staple for years. You can buy inferior brands for 99 cents at the discount store. During my eight-day Outward Bound trip in North Carolina, the only shelter was a huge blue tarp that could have covered the infield at Fenway Park. Our group would string a line between trees, fold the tarp over, and crawl under for the night. The rock, paper, scissors loser would be the tarp carrier for the day. Back home the cobalt cover could be used to cover outdoor grills, leaky roofs, or frost- fearing tomato plants. One could even put the family jewelry under a blue tarp in the back yard, since it was well known that no honorable thief in Maine would dare remove an item guarded in this fashion.

Finally, there is my beloved #27 butterfly needle. To my knowledge it is the tiniest available for general medical use. It looks like a piece of model railroad equipment. Before retirement, this #27 was kept in my wallet, still in its envelope, tucked underneath my license. If I were unable to find a usable arm or leg vein on a sick baby or small infant, there were usually a few small scalp veins which might accept this tiny needle. These intravenous lines were not very stable, but they always lasted long enough to administer initial doses of fluids, sugar or antibiotics.

These wee needles were often difficult to find in emergencies. "We didn't order anymore. Nobody uses them," the nurse would explain. I would then smile while reaching for my wallet.

However, when the police pull you over for a burned-out taillight, make certain that the needle doesn't flip out towards the officer as you pull out your license. Also, don't bring butterfly needles to the airport. The Transportation Security Authority would never understand.

Pictured: Christopher Moore on Mt. Katahdin Trip

LOOKIN' SHARP

Needles and syringes have played a vital role in the advancement of pediatrics. Most screaming infants and children do not share in this enthusiasm. "No shots today", are often the only words spoken as a small patient tiptoes into the exam room.

Primitive instruments for accessing the circulatory system were available as early as 1670, and in 1853 Charles Pravaz and Alexander Wood produced a needle sharp enough to pierce the skin easily. Early in the last century, the Becton Dickinson Company offered more advanced needles and syringes.

Improper needle sterilization caused a New Jersey hepatitis epidemic in the 1950s, demonstrating once again the need for disposable equipment. With a swift response, Becton Dickinson developed individual single needle and syringe units for polio vaccine administration. Glass syringes yielded to polypropylene plastic. The company soon went public to raise the money for the massive conversion to single use needles.

I began my medical career just as disposable needles became available, in short supply. Prior to this time needles were reground and sterilized for multiple uses. An intern needed the eagle eye of gemologist to spot tiny burrs on needle tips. The sharper ones were hidden away and saved for the sickest patients. Care for a spinal tap with a "kind of" sharp needle?

A resident physician with military experience volunteered to solve this shortage. It was rumored that the medical storeroom in a city hospital in New York contained pallets of the new disposable needles - which for some unknown reason were not available to the doctors in training. Under the cover of night he entered the storeroom and escaped with a box of the new needles. Supposedly, he led a security guard on a rooftop chase. The administration knew of the theft but could not find the booty. I could imagine the following conversation between two interns.

"Psst! I need a couple of disposable needles to start an intravenous on an elderly patient with terrible veins."

"I'll give you four twenty-one gauge, if you cover me next week for a few hours while I take my girlfriend out for her birthday dinner."

"Deal."

The following year when I was an intern in Boston, I was called in to see my boss, the Chief of Medicine. He was my idol, but was a large imposing figure with a stern voice. I feared the worst.

"Dr. Moore, We know about them."

"Sir, what are them?"

"Don't be coy."

"Sir?"

"The needles. The disposable needles. We know you have them. Where did you get them?"

"Ah, a friend . . . .ah, sir, I have a friend who is a salesman. He gave me a box of his company's new disposable needles. They are directly from the factory; sterile and in their wrappers. He wanted to get my opinion. They were free. I am actually saving the hospital money. Patients have been healed."

"Dr. Moore, you didn't clear this with us. Please bring me the box and don't do anything like this again. Your diploma depends upon it. Thank you."

Jimmy was a hemophiliac under my care during residency training. He was a likable child who tolerated his infusions well. Today, with artificial clotting compounds, we can teach the kids to perform their own intravenous treatments-even giving them prophylactically.

One winter evening Jimmy was brought from the ER to the ward with bleeding under his tongue. In those days, the ER resident always liked to clear the decks and get sick kids quickly upstairs-no longer their responsibility.

On my ward Jimmy was starting to gurgle as the hematoma under the tongue grew in size. Both he and mother had looks of horror on their faces. Jimmy had never before bled in this area. There was the terrifying thought of trying to force a breathing tube past the swollen tongue or attempting a tracheotomy – in a child who couldn't clot. In the treatment room the intravenous was started. Jimmy had a bad history of unsuccessful intravenous attempts.

It was a Catch 22. One needed the IV to administer the

clotting Factor 8. But, by inserting the needle, the vein might be just be traumatized enough to cause bleeding – even with a clean stick. Often a nurse would catch me at the door -

"Oh doctor. Before you go home I'd like to bring to your attention that hard blue lump around your needle tip." Notice again that any problem becomes MY problem. OUR is reserved for when things are going well.

Now, it was just Jimmy, mom, the nurse and I. The chief resident was attending an emergency. The attending doctor was at home. The wind started to howl and sleet rattled the windows. Yes, I do remember the scene exactly. Mother began to sob. I almost joined her. Jimmy was quiet. Christmas music wafted towards us from a radio down the hall.

After about ten minutes Jimmy's breathing became less labored. I was afraid to look at the butterfly needle tip, but the vial of clotting factor was dripping quickly into Jimmy's vein. Finally the nurse spoke up.

" The IV looks good. I think we did it."

Slowly over the next hour the swelling subsided and Jimmy's tongue looked less amphibian. Jimmy asked for some ice cream.

WHAT'S IN A NAME?

In medical jargon, LMD stands for local medical doctor. The term is generally used in mildly denigrating fashion, damning the subject with faint praise.

"Hey Dr. Moore," the nurse announced. "The LMD sent this baby in with a ductus."

It was the cardiology clinic during my residency. The ductus is a connection between the aorta and the lung artery. It opens during fetal life to direct blood into the aorta away from the lungs. It needs to close shortly after birth to supply blood to the now functioning lungs. If it fails to close, problems will slowly develop. You will also hear a blowing murmur under the left collarbone. I fully expected a normal exam. But no, the telltale murmur swished loudly under the baby's left clavicle. The LMD was correct. It suddenly dawned on me that next year in Maine, I would be the LMD.

Every medical school features a handful of brilliant students at the top of the class, but the rest are not far behind. I tutored several classmates who later became full professors and published articles in major medical journals. I, in turn, was tutored by other students. Some opted to practice academic medicine in large hospitals. Others of us wandered into more rural areas. Several local family practitioners in my area have made brilliant pediatric diagnoses. I view them as equals.

As an LMD I have encountered prejudice and skepticism. It was usually the resident physicians who were suspicious of us. The professors themselves were usually very kind and supportive. They helped me out on many occasions with their astute diagnoses. But I did hear a story of a Boston academic pediatrician saying that doctors were "doing things differently out west", referring to Worcester, Massachusetts.

Several years ago I submitted a case report to a prestigious pediatric journal. It concerned an adolescent who became quite ill from a rare bacterial infection contracted from fresh water swimming. My report was rejected because it "contributed nothing new to the pediatric literature." A review of the preceding twelve issues of this journal showed that none of the articles had been written by physicians who were not hospital-employed.

On a few occasions before modern scanning machines, I would send children to a medical center with a specific, correct, and urgent diagnosis only to receive the report back that the LMD found only vomiting or headache.

Another time our small hospital transferred a newborn with a rare bladder problem to Boston. A delayed diagnosis would have been fatal. The specialists were astounded that the LMDs of the woods were able to spot the problem so early.

The Academy of Pediatrics has recently championed a *brand new* concept of a "medical home" for all children. This is not a physical location but a concept in care. Every child should have access to family- supportive, compassionate, culturally appropriate care - even on nights and weekends. The pediatricians in our area have been doing this for decades - often with an in-office social worker. We labeled this endeavor "normal office hours". A hospital ad in our newspaper featured "new weekend outpatient hour". Saturday and Sunday morning office hours have been a rite of passage for many local baby doctors for years.

Some doctors are the PCP. When I first heard of this acronym it sounded like an oil additive, but it stands for primary care physician. The final P has unfortunately morphed from physician to provider. I suspect the insurance industry of coining this odious label. A recent article in a major pediatric journal described a questionnaire given to parents in the waiting room. "Please complete the following survey. Your provider would like to know how your child is doing."

Provider of what? Lawn service? Pest control? When signing forms, I always gleefully and forcefully scribble out the word provider and insert physician or doctor. "Well, Provider. Do you think my child will survive this illness?"

We all earned the title of doctor, just as nurses earned their RN. We both sit up all night with sick patients, miss school plays and weep at funerals. Even during time off we worry. We call to ask about patients from distant vacation spots. We find joy at birth and tears when grandparents die. We watch many brilliant dawns driving home from the hospital. We are much more than providers.

BEATS ME

One of the most difficult situations in medicine or life is to look a questioner straight in the eye and proclaim "I haven't got a clue."

My initial deployment of this plea was in college during my final exam in Russian Civilization 101. Are oral finals still in vogue? They were popular fifty years ago. The professor wished to see you in the flesh. My examiner had just returned from thirteen years at the American Embassy in Moscow. There would be no bluffing.

"Mr. Moore. Here is an outline of Europe. Pretend it is 1819. Just take my pointer and draw in the borders as they were then."

"Sir, another question?"

"What?"

"Sir. I haven't a clue."

"Really?"

"Really."

"Well, I know you have been accepted to medical school. And, you have attended all my lectures and passed the quizzes. I also know you can't flunk this test."

"Thank you."

National Medical Board tests were given in several stages. Passing these certified you to bypass state exams and directly obtain your state license. Part two was given at the end of your internship. There were questions about all the specialties - including the practical management of patients.

You were presented with a variety of imaginary patients with various histories, symptoms, and test results. Like a lottery scratch ticket, the test featured an erasable surface, and you would begin by rubbing off your best course of action. The answer underneath would give you more information or direction. The rotating internship, where young doctors were exposed to all of the specialties, was slowly disappearing, but these interns had a huge advantage in answering a broad range of medical questions. We budding internists had forgotten what a diaper or scalpel looked like.

Throughout the hall the sound of scrubbing erasers and four letter words filled the air. It soon became clear that your score would be inversely proportional to the number of erased squares. My Waterloo was the intoxicated college student who came back to his dorm late at night. He mistook the bathroom bottle of wintergreen oil for crème de menthe. Wintergreen is almost pure aspirin. As an internist in training, my knowledge of aspirin poisoning was poor. I should have thrown up the white flag and gone on to the next question.

But no. Over the next ten minutes the unlucky student died at least three times. A pile of shavings sat on my paper. Various warnings appeared as each incorrect answer was scrubbed away ... *Patient worsens ... Start over ... Do you really want to give this drug?* Would the Academy of Pediatrics eventually discover my crème de menthe fiasco? I was never able to sip this cloying digest without remembering this poor student.

Humility also paid dividends during the Pediatric Board oral exams. It was rumored that the year before I sat for this test, a top candidate was rejected because he seemed cocky and argumentative. For one part of the exam, a professor flipped though dozens of oversized medical photos on a large easel. You were supposed to shout out a diagnosis as quickly as you could. What had been a serious proceeding suddenly took on the air of a TV game show. I knew most of these diseases, but if there were any doubts I would answer "No idea, sir", with extra verve. The examiner seemed pleased.

I was certainly clueless when I saw my first patient as a medical student attending the New York Hospital Pediatric Clinic. One-year-old Juan was brought to the hospital because he had stopped walking. My knowledge base for sick children was sketchy, but Juan did not appear ill. He had no fever but refused to bear weight. There was concern about the possibility of a congenitally dislocated hip, but this exam was normal. Juan's x-ray and blood count were unrevealing.

I hadn't a clue what to do. Internists do a cardiogram when they didn't know what to do next. My brain vaguely recalled that pediatricians in a similar bind might place a skin test for tuberculosis. It gives the doctor a three-day grace period to think.

Experience later taught me to never allow a family to leave the office without something in their hands. It could be a Tylenol sample, some band-aids, an instruction sheet or in this case tuberculosis test. It's just good karma. My plan for Juan was approved by the attending physician, I think. Juan's tuberculosis test was a good-faith indicator that we were thinking about his problem. The family was asked to return in three days. In my heart of hearts I thought the skin test would be negative and Juan would magically walk back into the clinic, smiling.

Juan returned to the clinic two days later with a red and swollen test the size of a golf ball. Our initial x-ray had just missed showing the collapsed vertebrae above his hip. Juan had tuberculosis of the spine, brain, and lungs.

Our patient slowly recovered after weeks of intravenous antibiotics. His grandmother was sitting at home with open cavitary tuberculosis. She had infected most of the family. We were lucky. Often children with extensive tuberculosis are too sick to have a positive test. I learned to always be prepared for uncommon presentations of common diseases.

BRANDED

In the mid-1990s, the medical scene for physicians flying alone was a perfect storm of negative trends. The cost of running an office had skyrocketed. The number of Medicaid children in my practice had risen sharply. The payments from the state covered my overhead but there was nothing left over. This combination might have been sustainable, but malpractice insurance premiums had increased fifty-fold, and because of lawsuits, vaccine prices had gone over the top. Medical insurance at that time covered procedures or hospital fees, but not office visits. I often joked, with a grain of truth that you were not a true solo practitioner unless you had charged the payroll to your credit card a few times. But just like the bumblebee whose flight defies aeronautical physics, we kept the practice above water.

A group of solo pediatricians met to see if we might form a loose association to bargain with insurance companies and vendors for a better deal. Unknown to us, the internists and family practitioners were meeting secretly to forge a similar plan. Unable to unify the baby doctors, I joined the competing group as the lone pediatrician. Our local hospital hired a national accounting firm and off we went to form the first large multi-specialty doctor group in Maine. During this process, I and other members of our fledgling group attended conferences in distant cities where experts predicted supposed upcoming changes in medical practice. Many forecasts proved to be bogus. At a coffee break in a meeting in Atlanta, I questioned two members of n eight doctor pediatric group from California.

"How do you all get along? That's been a problem for me even in small groups."

"Well, Dr. Moore, actually we don't."

"Don't what?"

"We don't get along with each other. Actually, dislike would be the correct word."

"Do you see each other socially? Do the wives get along?"

"No and no, Dr. Moore."

"Why do you stay together?"

"We're only on call every eight days and the money is fantastic."

"I couldn't do that," I retorted.

"Oh yes you could."

Over time our organization morphed into shape. It was a humbling journey, one that medical school certainly had not prepared me for. Membership in our group was offered to any financially stable doctor who used the local hospital, and half accepted. For several years, many of my families refused to call the practice by its corporate name, which was understandable. Our office remained in the same physical location so the transition went fairly smoothly. The good news was that our office was placed on a budget and I received a paycheck, health insurance, and contributions to a retirement fund. Wendy no longer had to scramble for payroll.

We also built ancillary services such as laboratory and radiology. Profits from these units were used to care for under or uninsured children. Both doctors and patients were to be "branded" with the practice logo and the majority of medical dealings were to be kept within the corporate corral. As the practice grew we added several excellent female pediatricians who brought a new dimension to the office. I learned a great deal from them.

Consultants kept track of the "cowboys", the physician who joined the group reluctantly, retained some independent thinking, and pushed back against certain medical decisions filtering down from the top. As a group founder I would usually tow the party line, but on occasion I would be the doctor with horse, saddle, and hat. In a multi-specialty group, rules and regulations are not always child-friendly. Children are not small adults. The sticking points were very mundane – how to handle lunch hour, what time to leave the office at night, and do you want your pediatrician doing a Sunday kindergarten physical when she has been up all night with a sick newborn?

Our practice moved into a new building six months before my retirement. The change was bittersweet. My old cinder block office was showing the wear of several hundred thousand child visits over thirty years, but it was homey and located in the shadow of the hospital. The new facility was a half mile down the road and it housed several other specialties the lab, and the x-ray. The examining rooms were spacious and in compliance with disability regulations. On the other hand my new office was minuscule and no longer contained a couch for lunchtime renovation. To get around this, I would occasionally nap on our pricey new gynecological table.

Some families loved the new office; others preferred the converted snowmobile shop. The variety of opinions was akin to stances taken during the current health care debate. Those who favored the fresh new building, electronic prescriptions, and one stop lab/x-ray were balanced by those who liked the cozier "mom and pop" milieu. These traditionalists sometimes authored clever variations of the corporate name and sometimes voted with their feet.

Gaily painted jungle animals prowled the new waiting and exam rooms. Our medical assistants lost their offices also and were now lined up along a long counter. Pediatrics shifted to the second floor which was serviced by a large elevator. I was always terrified that one of my hyperactive patients might jam the elevator between floors.

Just as I retired, my twelve year old medical group was purchased by our local hospital. Our laboratory and radiology services, whose profits underwrote uninsured patients, came into direct competition with the hospital. The community could not support both, and our group would lose in a shootout. A compromise was reached. The good news for our now hospital-based doctors was they would now be paid a flat amount for each patient seen, regardless of the family's ability to pay. The hospital would become the payer of last resort. I commend them for this attempt to provide care for all in our community- but they will need more numbers of insured patients for their altruism to continue.

PAPERLESS

Late in my career, our physician's group switched to electronic medical records. I had zero training in computers along my medical path.

In 1960 we had a teaching aid in medical school that was probably a forerunner of today's computer. It was the size of a TV and taught us parasitology. My cell phone probably has 1000 times the capacity of this primitive instrument. Two of my children now make their livelihoods from computer-related jobs that didn't exist when they were in college. In the early 1980s, my third son, David, purchased a new Commodore 64 and dabbled with programs that were saved with a cassette recorder. It now sits quietly in our basement. I am hoping for a revival on eBay.

Wendy first used an Apple system for our office accounts in the 1990s. There were ups and downs. Sometimes, on Sunday evenings, I could hear her alternately laughing and crying with their excellent support group in Nebraska. In retirement it held our Christmas card list.

Computer savvy doctors from our multispecialty group researched several systems for over a year. When the decision was made, two very kind technical support instructors from India struggled to get me on board. I wonder what they said in private about my profound ignorance.

The actual process of going online was challenging. There were promises from the medical systems company that an army of temporary employees would swoop in from parts unknown and within weeks convert our existing data. They never showed up. We tried to record the information from the most complicated patients first. Fitting this into our regular schedule was a daunting task. New babies and transfers entered the practice faster than we could eliminate paper charts. It was like a scene from the *Sorcerer's Apprentice.*

The advantages of electronic records were many. The screen was compact and legible. I could access records from home, which was invaluable, especially when dealing with patients of other pediatricians in our group. Allergies, family history and past hospitalizations were instantly noted and highlighted. I could make appointments and check my schedule. If admitting a youngster to the hospital or sending one to the emergency room, I could give the mother a printed copy of the office visit to take with her. I could finally send prescriptions electronically, and the pharmacist no longer had to guess at my handwriting, which, although not terrible for a physician, has been ridiculed by my family for years.

Prior to electronic records, dictated mini cassettes had to be delivered to the transcriptionist, who was in a distant location. Then the sticky progress notes had to be carefully pressed into the correct charts in the correct location, like a second grade project. Going digital removed the need for chart repair with glue, tape and three hole punches.

The downsides were plentiful also. The actual typing

was done by the physicians. I would be embarrassed to admit my typing speed. There were canned paragraphs where you just had to type in the positive findings. Some doctors have become skilled at voice to dictation programs like Dragon, but laryngitis and thick accents have caused weird translations.

I also had to enter in the diagnostic codes for billing. Like most items in medicine our system was not friendly to pediatricians. I had to carry around ten laminated sheets of diagnostic codes from the Academy of Pediatrics. I was delighted to find that the author of the code list had a wicked sense of humor. Hidden among the standard codes were the following –

ACCIDENTS: CHILD HIT BY DEBRIS FROM SPACECRAFT

MENTAL HEALTH: IRRITABLE PERSON

I triggered an inordinate number of freeze-ups and meltdowns in the middle of the morning, problems that never surfaced in the evening or at dawn. It gradually became apparent that our state of the art system was having heartburn at 10 A.M. trying to digest the entries of thirty doctors and more nurses, but nobody was quite willing to own up to the problem.

A strange problem involved electronic prescriptions. Sometimes my nurse or secretary would ask-

"Dr. Moore, the pharmacist from Megapharm called. You forgot to send Shawn's prescription electronically."

"Didn't they leave two minutes ago?" I would respond.

Either Shawn's mother had NASCAR driving talent or she had cell-phoned Granny, hovering at the drug store counter.

Finally, there was the time a family from Portland with a one-month old infant transferred into the practice. An inch-thick medical record accompanied the baby. My first thought was that this chart announced a child with a fantastically complicated history. I envisioned nights poring over arcane journals.

As I thumbed through the pages there were hundreds of medical history questions and answers. I was impressed with the thoroughness of the interview until I actually read it - "denies swollen legs, denies shortness of breath when climbing stairs, denies change in libido". Either this was a walking, talking, sexually active one-month old or else an employee had neglected to turn off a computer program before lunchtime.

Electronic records have the capability of producing significant progress in medical care. However, because of the high cost, many physician groups are awaiting less expensive or federally funded systems. New programs need to be user-friendly, fast and accurate. They must be able to handle peak loads and interface with other medical systems. I will continue after I get this screen unfrozen.

IMMUNIZE YOUR CHILDREN

The recent upsurge in anti-vaccination rhetoric must be answered with a calm presentation of medical facts. I was fortunate to practice pediatrics with the assistance of immunization, but I am old enough to remember a darker time.

I practiced for two years in the Air Force before the measles vaccine was formulated. During that time, I cared for several infants with permanent brain damage caused by this virus. In underdeveloped countries, measles still kills malnourished children. Measles epidemics sometimes spread from intentionally unvaccinated children to healthy toddlers who are not old enough to be vaccinated. The measles vaccine is effective - I have not seen a case in thirty years. During my training, we saw two children who were critically ill with inflamed hearts caused by chickenpox. They both survived thanks to large doses of cortisone, a difficult treatment. This virus can also attack the kidneys, brain, lungs and other organs. Half of all children with flesh-eating streptococcal skin infections start down that horrific path with infected chickenpox blisters. This virus can also cause severe disability and death. After the advent of the chickenpox vaccine, I rarely saw this disease.

Homophilus influenza group B (Hib) is an invasive bacteria that can cause life-threatening meningitis, deep eye infections, and severe swelling of the epiglottis (cover to the voice box). I vividly remember many patients who became severely ill with Hib disease. They numbered from six to eight per year during my first twenty years, but after the Hib vaccine became available in 1986, this disease disappeared from my practice. Unfortunately, our state is starting to see a resurgence of Hib disease in children who have not been immunized.

The list goes on: meningitis with mumps, damaged babies from rubella, dehydration from rotavirus diarrhea, spasms from tetanus, and deaths from whooping cough, polio, meningococcal disease and invasive pneumococci–all preventable with vaccination.

The anti-vaccination movement exploded in 1998 when British gastroenterologist Andrew Wakefield claimed to have found the measles virus in bowel biopsies of twelve autistic children who had recently received an MMR (measles, mumps, and rubella) vaccine. He felt this might explain the apparent rise in the number of autistic children. The findings were published in the prestigious medical journal *The Lancet*. Wakefield stated that one certain way to avoid an autistic child would be to forego the measles inoculation. This pronouncement hit the media like a bomb. Entire nations prohibited MMR. Opponents of vaccination appeared on the talk show circuit and in front of Congress.

In time, the connection between autism and MMR began to unravel. Researchers could not duplicate Wakefield's results. His assistant denied testing the biopsies for measles. The co-authors removed their names from the paper and later *The Lancet* rescinded the entire study. Finally, the most damning piece of evidence emerged. In those countries where measles vaccines had been discontinued, the incidence of autism had actually increased slightly. Ten later studies demonstrated no connection between MMR and autism.

During this time, some physicians and parents also became concerned about the amount of mercury that infants were receiving in the form of thiomerosal preservative n their vaccines. The story is complex and politically charged. The critics of thiomerosal talk about mercury, but not all mercury is the same.

You surely remember from high school chemistry that the methyl radical has one carbon surrounded by three hydrogen, and that the ethyl radical has two carbons. This tiny difference in chemical structure produces vastly different outcomes in the human body. For example, ethyl alcohol gives you a buzz, but methyl alcohol produces blindness.

Early in the last century, there was a deadly problem with bacterial contamination of multi-dose vaccine vials each time rubber stopper was punctured. When ethyl mercury was added, the pathogens disappeared. It seemed the ideal preservative. Ethyl mercury was combined with thiosalicylate to produce thiomerosal, which killed bacteria even better. When injected into animals at thousands of times the amount given to babies, it was shown to be non-toxic. Thiomerosal was even used to treat an outbreak of meningitis in 1929.

These doses were almost a million times higher than those found in vaccines - it was a poor antibiotic but it did not cause any harm.

213

Methyl mercury is the harmful form of mercury generated by coal-burning power plants. In large doses, it can be toxic. At the end of World War II methyl mercury contamination from a Japanese factory produced severe neurological damage and death in that community. But the poison did not produce autism.

Despite its excellent safety record, there was a push to eliminate thiomerosal and switch to single dose vaccines. This would increase the cost but was not a bad idea. Unfortunately, a poorly worded statement from the American Academy of Pediatrics and Public Health Service said that this would make the vaccines even safer. This implied that vaccines given in the first year of life were not fully safe to begin with. This confusing dictum caused some hospitals to forgo the first hepatitis B shot in the nursery. Babies around the country were needlessly infected by their mothers. Not only did the infants suffer liver damage but some died because of acute infection. As the safety of thiomerosal was questioned, some parents opted out of DPT and Hib vaccines. Predicable outbreaks of whooping cough and meningitis followed.

As one might expect from the MMR studies, the removal of thiomerosal from vaccines did not result in a decrease in new cases of autism or neurological disease. Several European nations had years ago removed this preservative; their autism rates actually increased. Six studies failed to prove a link between thiomerosal and autism.

The tide maybe turning. In early 2009 in Federal Claims Court, the three judge panel of the Omnibus Autism

Proceeding ruled in favor of the government in a class action suit via the National Childhood Vaccine Injury Act by parents who felt that a combination of MMR vaccine and thiomerosal preservative caused autism in their children. In March 2010 in the second phase, three Federal judges ruled in three separate cases that thiomerosal does not cause autism.

Your child's physician is in the best position to advise you. If immunization rates fall below certain levels we will start to see the reemergence of many life-threatening diseases.

TODD

"Todd's mom is on the phone for you," my secretary said softly with tears in her eyes.

We always remember our circumstances when bad news comes. I was at the back of the office, looking for a chart while glimpsing out at the bleak winter landscape.

Suicide is the third leading cause of death in older teens, taking thousands of lives each year. Risk factors include a chronic disease, drinking, depression, victims of bullying, and a family history of suicide.

Warning signs include insomnia, daytime sleeping, avoiding family gatherings, withdrawal from school, and a period of euphoria just before the final act. Todd had all of the above.

Todd's mother Christina was calling to tell me that Todd had taken his life that morning. Later, I would spend an hour or so talking with Christina and her father at his home.

Todd developed persistent asthma at a young age. This illness limited his ability to play outside with his friends and also led to intermittent treatment with prednisone. Both of these are risk factors for obesity. There are also links between obesity, asthma, and depression, which are not fully understood.

Christina remembers Todd as a compassionate and sensitive child. His father was not in the picture. Todd

217

enjoyed four-wheeling, hiking in the mountains, sitting on the beach, and teaching his black lab Sadie new tricks. He would take his younger brother out to Dairy Queen when a stressful event arose. Christina was a caring mother and never used physical punishment.

As Todd entered junior high school he endured taunts about his weight, dress and lisp. During his sophomore year, Todd dropped out of school – promising his mother he would get his GED by the time he was eighteen. He went to live with his grandfather in an adjacent town, to be close after his grandmother died. In time I was asked to treat Todd for depression. It didn't go well. He felt that the medication was not working, and there was a family history of a severe reaction to my second choice of anti-depressant. Ultimately, he did not want to be labeled as a mental health patient. In retrospect, I should have been more proactive about getting Todd back to the office after a number of missed appointments.

Then, as is often the case before a suicide, Todd went through several months in a better mood. He bonded with several Canadian friends he had met playing games online, and a few days before he died, they visited the Hockey Hall of Fame. Christina was pleased that Todd was losing weight.

Christina feels the pain daily. Back problems make it difficult to care for her other children, but she has gone forward with her life. She gathered with Todd's friends to celebrate what would have been his eighteenth birthday. Two years later, the Federal Drug Administration announced a possible link between one of Todd's asthma medications and suicide, a proclamation that remains highly controversial to this day.

Parents must be alert to the signs of a possible suicide - particularly insomnia, victimization by bullies, alcohol use and depression. Suicide does not automatically indicate a parenting failure or a character flaw in the victim. Suicide can strike anywhere, and is blind to income and education levels. Even medical and mental health professionals can miss warning signs in their own families and be blindsided. When outsiders make thoughtless and judgmental comments about a suicide, their words will augment the pain of the grieving family beyond description.

Christina feels that if one life can be altered by her story, Todd's death will have been worth her pain.

The National Suicide Prevention Hotline is:
1-800-273-8255

Pictured: Todd

RAISING READERS

Like many doctors, I have always been an avid reader. My sister, and then my family, quickly learned never to give me a book too early on Christmas Day - I would generally wander off until dinner. Over the years, it has been a privilege to attempt to help get more children interested in reading. A strong background in reading at a young age fosters creativity and intelligence. These skills will not only be crucial for work and family but, more importantly, for a general appreciation of life. A recent study found that it takes only ten children's books in a household to foster good reading habits.

The Libra Foundation, established by microchip heiress Elizabeth B. Noyce to promote general welfare in Maine, set up the Maine Raising Readers Program in 2003. The program provides each child in Maine with a free book at every check-up from the nursery through kindergarten. Maine writers are given special consideration. God forbid you should forget to hand over the book, as the child or parent will sternly remind you.

Often we take access to books for granted. Shortly after my arrival in Maine I was approached by a local librarian to help his brother, a pediatric surgeon in Kiev. This Russian doctor was not allowed to read international journals or medical books. How political could these be? We found funds through various sources and purchased an armful of recent texts and journals. My friend managed to smuggle a small library into the Soviet Union for his brother. Perhaps he put

War and Peace jackets on all of them. The recipient somehow managed to send back a grateful note. For several years I was fearful of unknown men in dark raincoats.

I participated in a state-wide book club for medical professionals sponsored by the Maine Humanities Council. Some of the chapters in this book were written as homework for our group of doctors, nurses and social workers. Book topics ranged from medieval plague to HIV. The program has gained national recognition. While discussing a book describing post traumatic stress syndrome after WWI, our group discovered that we had a WWII flight nurse and a Vietnam War medic in our midst. Another time, while the club members read a documentary about West Virginia silica lung disease, a participant volunteered she had grown up ten miles from the mine.

Shortly after arriving in Maine, I became involved with reading issues in our local schools. Ruth, a matronly reading teacher, delighted in lifting educationally challenged children towards literacy. Like the pied piper, she would roam the buildings, while trailing children would look for an opportunity to hop into her lap for a quick read. She was well versed in the newer reading research.

Some of the traditional teachers were upset because Ruth would take children from their homeroom classes for special reading help. Though I am not an educator, it seemed logical that if these students were not reading, time in the regular classroom would not be especially productive. We held workshops and brought in actual students with ADD, dyslexia, and other learning problems to graphically demonstrate their defects. I could hear some teachers grumbling in the background.

One year, Ruth focused on a classroom for developmentally delayed children, taught many to read, and then mainstreamed them back into regular classrooms. Today federal and state funding mandates that this problem is addressed early and with vigor.

Read to your children as early and as often as you can. If a child finds a book boring, the parents should simply suggest something else, without criticism. The cost of books can be addressed by trips to the library - which also sets the table for the importance of reading, library story time, and later use for finding reference material for school assignments. While girls may be drawn to themes of relationships, boys may find action or sports more appealing. All books for younger readers need strong characters and plot lines that move. Books in series are an excellent tool for fostering reading - if your child does not hook on the first book, try another series. Several years ago, a Hardy Boys volume was the only reading material available to me in a cabin. I read it cover to cover.

LITTLE WHITE LIES

In medicine and life, one is occasionally put in a position of having to stretch the truth just a bit. Or maybe leave out some information.

"Hey, Dr. Moore. I don't think the child is breathing," whispered the respiratory technician.

"Yeah, my thoughts were just the same."

The eight-year-old Massachusetts girl had been vacationing nearby with her family. Her bike collision with a car had rendered her unconscious. The transporting ambulance had decided to duck into our emergency room on the way to the medical center. The emergency medical technicians did not like her breathing.

A quick neurological exam yielded only a slight response to a hard pinch. Her pupils were equal but only sluggishly responsive to bright light. There was an obvious skull fracture, blood dribbling from her left ear, and her mouth was full of blood. The mother was frantically looking over my shoulder and quickly told me that she was an intensive care nurse in Boston. My luck was running its usual course.

The technician suctioned the child's mouth and ventilated her with full oxygen.

"I'm going to intubate your daughter to stabilize her airway for the rest of the ambulance ride."

"Yes, that's a good idea, doctor."

The mother was not told that her child was not breathing on her own. No doubt, she thought that I was an anesthesiologist or a critical care doctor. No time for that discussion. We did not have oxygen monitors at that time, which was good - we did not want to know the numbers. Intubation is often easy in a comatose child and that was the case here. My mind envisioned a damaged or deceased child. The trip to the medical center went well, and the neurosurgeon met us in the emergency room. We gave our report and returned home.

Daily reports came from the medical center and to my amazement, our biker made excellent progress. Her depressed skull fracture was elevated surgically but there seemed to be no damage to the brain itself. Later we learned she made a full recovery except for some hearing loss in the injured ear.

The mother sent me a thank you note. She never mentioned the intubation. The letter from a Boston law firm came shortly afterward. It was left unopened for a while on my desk as bad thoughts danced in my mind. The envelope was of parchment quality with the name of all the law partners listed in calligraphic style, as if the Declaration of Independence might be inside. The lawyers wished more medical information. That could be done. No letters followed, probably indicating a lawsuit against the driver of the car.

Another little white lie concerned my first malpractice policy, which I found in a box of old files the other day.

226

The fee for this insurance was ninety-eight dollars per year, the equivalent of a mortgage payment. Today malpractice costs a year of mortgage payments. The policy also contained tips for staying free of lawsuits.

The list contained such sage advice as wash your hands, clean your instruments, be nice to people, document each visit, and . . . never, ever tell anybody that you carry malpractice insurance. Disclosing that fact to families would only release a maelstrom of litigation. This would be bad for you and your insurance company. Thank you, have a nice day.

During my internship I had the privilege of caring for Dorothy, a lovely senior admitted with pneumonia from a very substandard nursing home. Dorothy responded to our treatment and after a week, it was time to return. Several interns and residents, however, insisted she deserved a better long-term care situation. Thusly, we devised a holding pattern plan while exploring alternate placements. We stretched our patient's diagnosis of occasional heartburn into a more ominous sounding erosive esophagitis, and then ordered an upper gastrointestinal contrast x-ray. Yes, that's when you drink the yuckie-tasting chalky frappe and they take movies of your stomach. Yes, and you remember that you can't eat or drink overnight. Yes, you can guess what we did.

"Doctor, Mrs. Smith is scheduled for an upper GI series today. She shouldn't have breakfast."

"Thank you, nurse, 'wink, wink'. But please read the order sheet."

Then sometime later –

"Dr. Moore, this is the x-ray technician. Your patient had breakfast. The radiologist says the study can't be done. Please reschedule."

"I'm sorry. Thank you. We will reschedule."

And reschedule we did – several times for several tests.

Finally, one morning a strange man in a suit arrived at the nursing station, asking to talk with the interns.

"Gentlemen. I am from administration. We are on to your little game with Mrs. Smith. Please discharge her today. Your diploma depends upon it. Thank you."

Mrs. Smith was discharged to another nursing home. I was on different ward later in the year when word filtered back. The house staff was not entirely happy with this new location. Somehow, they pulled strings and Mrs. Smith was brought back to city hospital by ambulance during a heat wave. Her diagnosis was chronic vitamin deficiency.

Sometimes small fibs are used for worthwhile endeavors. In 2004, the hospital medical director asked me to join him the next day for lunch. He wanted to pick my brain about some medical problem. That seemed strange. He knew more pediatrics than I did and it seemed that we could do this over the phone. Oh well. On arrival, I was ushered into a conference room with a few dozen-hospital higher-ups and a buffet. Hmm. Would I have to offer pediatric advice to everyone. Why were they all assembled? As I pondered this, the crowd seemed to be slowly inching forward and encircling me. I actually thought for a moment it was a Betty Ford confrontation. I was to lose my hospital privileges because of deteriorating handwriting or unfinished charts. It seemed a bit harsh. The director started speaking - about the hospital award I was to receive. In truth, the citation belonged to all who helped care for children in our hospital or office - from custodians to secretaries to technicians to nurses.

The last story involves yours truly again. For obvious reasons, physicians are terrible patients. When their own medical care is involved they are sometimes arrogant, foolish, and in denial - I might be the poster child. One December night in 1996, I experienced some mild right neck and shoulder pain while coughing with a respiratory infection. In this case, the American Heart Association urges you to call 911. I was certain that my discomfort was either one of my common neck migraines or the old football shoulder, and popped a few Advil.

After a number of hours without relief, a visit to our local emergency room seemed in order. It was now 5AM on a Sunday. Leaving Wendy a bogus note about going to the office to do some paper work, I actually called the ER to make certain that they were not too busy- then headed north.

The denial continued in the hospital as the doctors ordered a chest x-ray because of my coughing. Finally, a nurse friend of mine said, "We've been pissing around too long here." Making the correct diagnosis of myocardial infarction, she gently shoved an oxygen tube up my nose and put nitroglycerin paste onto my chest.

Several days later, I was recovering at the medical center after receiving a coronary stent. My roommate was a good old boy from New Hampshire who was one of the last remaining craftsmen of birch bark canoes. He looked like Santa and was outrageously funny.

When I told my new friend about my Advil failure, he responded, "Yeah. I found that Pepcid AC don't do bleep for a heart attack either."

SAMMY

"I've just fired my pediatrician, Dr. Moore. You are now the one."

Anxiety surrounds this situation. First, I may not have anything new or creative to add to the child's diagnosis or treatment. Secondly, would my style of doctoring fit with this new family? I have long since ceased trying to figure out why families transfer in or out of a practice. Sometimes it's straightforward - a missed diagnosis, a bad outcome, or one of my grumpy days. At times there is feedback, other times not. A child whose life was saved is transferred out. A patient whose family we reported for possible child abuse stays in. Who can figure?

My new patient's history was fascinating. He had suddenly developed symptoms of severe obsessive-compulsive disorder. He repeated movements, exited the house only by the rear door, and had great difficulty changing tasks. The list went on and on. His mother, Beth, at first attributed the strange behavior to a move to a new house but it soon became clear that something more ominous was at hand. There was little, if any, history of mental illness.

There can be a variety of causes for the sudden onset of mental illness. I have cared for children with medical problems, such as brain abscess, lead poisoning, and low thyroid, who have shown acute behavior disturbance. Other times external forces may do the same - the suddenly mute girl whose father was sexually abusing her. Why does the non-drug using college student awaken one morning to find himself psychotic? When psychiatric disease occurs abruptly and without significant family history, a red flag is waving for the doctor.

One of Beth's friends suggest that she investigate strep. This woman's child had obsessive-compulsive behavior (OCD) and increased streptococcal antibodies. Pediatric Autoimmune Neuropsychiatric Disorders Associated with Streptococcal Infections, or PANDAS syndrome, is thought by some physicians to be a legitimate link between these two entities, but there is controversy. My residency training provided hands-on experience in treating children with chorea, a brain disorder causing involuntary writhing movement of the extremities, following streptococcal throat infections. It is but a short leap to imagine the body's immune system mistaking the tissue in other brain areas for the surface of strep bacteria.

Beth began her odyssey. Being a lawyer specializing in the rights of children in the court system gave her a clear advantage when advocating for Sammy. She rarely took "no" for answer and could understand the pediatric literature. I heard a discussion of PANDAS in 2001 at the annual pediatric seminar given by Phoenix Children's Hospital. It seemed to have some legitimacy.

Meanwhile Sammy was deteriorating. He would spend hours in one spot. There were several times when he refused to leave the car to enter my office.

We obtained the first set of anti-strep antibodies on Sammy. They were elevated. Beth was ecstatic. We started penicillin. By the fifth day, Sammy had stopped his repetitive movements and speech. Even Sammy said he was "full of hope". On the eighteenth day Sammy went back to school.

Beth contacted a reporter from the Boston Globe. He did an interview, which appeared in the paper shortly afterward. Beth received a flood of e-mail from parents of children with OCD. Some had never heard of PANDAS. Others had children who had responded to antibiotics or extreme blood cleansing procedures.

The story does not end happily quite here, however. After a month the penicillin stopped working. The stiffness, tics, and OCD symptoms were back. Sammy's anti-strep antibodies were elevated. A variety of other antibiotics were tried without success. During our season of despair, I told Beth about the Australian pathologist Dr. J. Robin Warren. He thought that the H. pylori bacteria were the cause of peptic ulcer disease. The medical world thought he was crazy. Years later, when his theory proved correct, he was awarded a Noble Prize in Medicine.

Beth found the name of the New Jersey specialist who was treating her friend's son for PANDAS. To her amazement, Beth discovered that Dr Catherine Nicolaides had treated a number of patients with presumed PANDAS with Augmentin – a stronger cousin of the common antibiotic amoxicillin.

Getting Sammy to New Jersey was akin to the Lewis and Clark expedition. The motel room had to be on the first floor or have an elevator. Moving Sammy in and out of

233

the van took hours. Dr. Nicolaides finally saw Sammy and started the Augmentin. There seemed to be slow improvement. When symptoms flared, Dr. Nicolaides and Beth would increase the Augmentin to high levels for a week or so. Sammy's speech and cognition improved. He was able to relate his medical journey in a moving speech at his Bar Mitzvah. Beth began working with a psychiatrist at Massachusetts General Hospital. Sammy was gradually weaned from his low-dose OCD meds. Beth adjusted his Augmentin as needed.

In 2004 Sammy won the Southern Maine Math League competition. He defeated 600 other students and was chosen to attend the prestigious and elite Maine School of Science and Mathematics. He is now attending Carnegie Mellon University. Beth's book *Saving Sammy* was released by Random House in September 2009. She has since participated in a variety of media interviews and her home video of Sammy's worst moments was shown on the Today Show.

Though the relationship between strep infections and sudden-onset OCD remains controversial, there are increasing numbers of these patients who improve with antibiotic or blood cleansing treatment. Ongoing research will obviously shed more light on neuropsychiatric disorders in children. While the puzzle of mental disease awaits completion, parents and physicians should look carefully for medical causes of sudden-onset psychiatric disease in children, especially if the symptoms involve abnormal muscle movement.

For more information log on to:
www.pandasfoundation.org.

IT HURTS RIGHT HERE, DOCTOR

In the old days if you had lower abdominal pain on the right side, tenderness, an elevated white blood count and a fever, your appendix was quickly removed. There was probably a ten to fifteen percent chance that you were fine and had undergone an unnecessary procedure. Today with computerized tomography and sophisticated blood tests, the odds are better. A few stories come to mind, but first some background.

Only humans, chimps, gorillas, orangutans, gibbons, and wombats have an appendix. Andreas Vesalius and Gabriele Fallopio likened this pouch to a worm in the 1500s. There was confusion over the next several centuries as to whether this worm causes abdominal abscesses or is just an innocent bystander. Standard treatment included the swallowing of lead, mercury, laxatives, and opiates. Also touted was the use of recently killed small animals, the avoidance of heat, and massage. Sometimes, but not often, the patient would survive.

In 1889, Charles McBurney wrote his famous paper locating the pain of acute appendicitis exactly two-thirds of the way from the belly button to the right hip. Were that always the case. Dr. Thomas Morton is credited for performing the first standard appendectomy in 1882. The patient was a 26-year-old paperhanger who had developed an appendiceal abscess. When leeches failed, a standard incision was made, pus drained, and the offending organ ligated and removed. Anesthesia consisted of an ounce of whiskey. The patient miraculously recovered.

The most famous appendectomy caused the temporary postponement of Edward's 1902 coronation. The monarch in waiting wished to wait a while and see how his lower abdominal pain progressed. His surgeon, Dr. Frederick Treves, was said to have answered, 'Sir, I know the answer. You will leave the palace as a corpse." Because of improved anesthesia, antiseptic solutions, and a skilled surgeon, the king survived and was crowned two months later.

In the days before scans and rapid pregnancy tests, teens with early-undiagnosed pregnancies sometimes went under the knife. Whoever drew the short straw had to relay the news, good and bad, to the anxious parents in the waiting room.

If the patient has a concurrent disease, appendicitis can be tricky to discern. One patient of mine was already in the hospital for an infected ankle. He then developed pain around the right kidney. I was led astray by the history of a prior kidney infection in the year before. By the time, I realized the problem was an abnormally positioned appendix, it had ruptured. In retrospect, I chose the correct antibiotic for the infected ankle, but not for quieting a hot appendix.

The strangest case involved my secretary's son. Eddie arrived with severe *left* lower abdominal pain. In the hospital, he required substantial narcotic doses for comfort. After x-rays and blood tests were inconclusive, his surgeon and I opted for a look through the laparoscope. The appendix looked normal but there was excessive fluid in the abdomen. The incision was enlarged to several inches and we visually inspected the whole bowel, but found nothing unusual. Following protocol, we removed the normal appendix. I apologized profusely to mother but then retracted my statement when we found evidence of appendicitis on the microscopic sections.

As is often the case, my own appendix pain started up under the lower breastbone. It felt like what ulcer pain must feel like. I was taken to the emergency room at 3 A.M. by a friend who is a policeman because I didn't wish to tie up an ambulance. The discomfort moved lower. Not wishing to awaken the surgeon at that hour, I conspired with nurses. We started an IV, got me admitted, and ordered a blood count. When the doctor came in at 7 A.M., he confessed he had a dream that I had come to the ER. The staff denied that they had called him in the night.

It sounds weird, but appendicitis is hereditary , and I passed it along to two of my sons. When Christopher was in medical school, he was admitted to the university hospital because of abdominal pain. Eventually he was seen by the chief of surgery who felt his problem was not worthy of an operation. He was then seen in follow-up by a medical resident from a foreign country who checked my son for parasites. Christopher then noticed his waistline expanding visibly, but decided to go to a wedding in the Midwest. When he got back to Baltimore, he looked like the Michelin tire man. He called on a Friday night.

"Hey Dad, I still don't feel right."

"Do you have any belly pain?"

"I'm not sure."

"Jump up and down."

"Yeah, that hurts."

"Do you have a fever?"

"Not sure", he answered.

"Find out."

He called back five minutes later. "105 degrees."

"Call the emergency room. Tell them you are coming by cab and need to see your surgeon. No more parasite tests. It's late fall in Baltimore. The worms have all gone south for the winter."

He called back three minutes later.

"Doc, they said I can't go to the hospital. There's a citywide gang war tonight. Everything is on red alert and locked down."

Christopher was seen as soon as the blockade was lifted. It took the surgeon almost an hour to find his appendix as it was plastered onto the backside of his bladder. After two weeks in the hospital, he was only partially healed. We needed a wheelchair to fly him back to Maine to finish his convalescence. He had lost twenty-five pounds. Wendy's home cooking started him on the path to recovery, and he was able to run the Boston Marathon next spring.

Some years later my third son David called from Boston. He had right lower abdominal pain and vomiting, but wanted my blessing to leave town for the weekend.

Fool me twice, shame on me.

"David. Listen up. You are a healthy male. There is nothing but an appendix in your right lower abdomen. No ovary. No uterus. Probably no kidney. No nothing. Unpack your suitcase. Call your doctor. Then call me. Thank you."

David did as told and his inflamed appendix was removed later that day.

OUT OF THE MOUTHS OF BABES

Barbara Bush honored our office in 2007 by handing out the one-millionth book of the Raising Readers program. The recipient was five-year-old Jacob, who of course stole the show in front of the TV cameras. After his monologue, Mrs. Bush said "I would like to take you home with me."

"I can't do that", answered Jacob. "I already have a family."

Sometimes my patients will directly question my competence. Matt was in for his kindergarten physical. I will often weave a reading readiness test into the conversation. What color is grass? Draw a square. Does Christmas come in summer or winter? What color is the sky? Matt seemed unimpressed with the whole process.

At supper, Matt's father asked what had transpired during the physical. Matt shrugged his shoulders and answered.

"Dr. Moore isn't very smart. He asked me a lot of simple questions that he didn't know the answers to."

Though officially finished with office practice, I try to do some volunteer work. Retired husbands need to give their wives some space and time alone on a regular basis. The following conversation took place as I was administering flu vaccines at a local school. I recognized a former patient. The slightly nervous second grader scanned my face for several moments. Then with a puzzled voice, she issued the following declaration.

241

"You look just my old doctor, but he died."

I must have been looking ghostly that week because few days later the high school flu clinic prompted this exchange.

"I can't believe you are a senior in high school."

"I can't believe you are still alive, Dr. Moore!"

Another time I was babysitting a four-year-old child who had to use a public restroom. Declining assistance, he asked me just to guard the door.

Several silent minutes went by. I feared the youngster had been swallowed by the toilet.

"Are you OK? Say something."

"Employees must wash hands before returning to work!"

One aid to help with the diagnosis of attention deficit hyperactive disorder is the continuance performance test. The test is a toaster-sized metal box with three small windows in the front, just like a slot machine. Random digits flash in the center window. When a certain sequence appears , the youngster is supposed to push the red button on top of the box. Failure to recognize the sequence or the use of excessive force on the button suggests an attention problem, but of course, there were responses not covered in the instruction manual.

Several children, after a few minutes, abruptly left the room while muttering, "I don't like this exercise."

Another child attempted to disassemble the device, finally asking for a screwdriver. Yet another patient held the button down continuously. By far the strangest result of all test was the child who suddenly abandoned the test, jumped onto the exam table and sang a verse of *Auld Lang Syne*. It may surprise you to learn that not all of these children turned out to have attention issues.

One boy at the residential treatment center was having a bad mental health day. We usually had a good relationship but during this visit, I didn't quite tune into his mood.

"Hi, Jonathan, how are you doing?"

"Bleep you, Dr. Moore!"

To the credit of the institution, the child apologized immediately and I received weekly letters of apology until his discharge.

CELEBRATION OF LIFE

During my career, I had the honor of being invited by former patients to countless birthdays, graduations, and weddings.

My favorite birthday was Marc's fortieth. My friend had endured the challenges of Down syndrome with courage and humor. He gave me a big smile and wave from across county club lobby as I approached in costume wearing a surgical mask and a stethoscope.

Graduations are always special, especially when someone I have taken care of makes it all the way through medical school.

The teen girl who appears in the *A Disease Too Soon* chapter was accepted to an Ivy League school. Because I had interviewed her for the institution, she returned to tell me that she was, to my astonishment, accepting a spot at a Bible college in the Deep South. She hoped I wasn't upset, but in the back of my mind, I immediately understood that cost might have been a factor. We looked eye to eye and I solemnly made her promise to follow through on her dream of becoming a physician. She said yes.

Eight years later, her graduation announcement from a Midwest medical school lay on my desk. If the school had been just a bit closer, I would have attended.

Several years later, my friend stopped by the office to say hello. She was now a surgical resident at a teaching hospital.

I also had the honor of participating in a medical school graduation *hooding* ceremony (the new doctor receives his academic hood and recites the Hippocratic Oath) for a local osteopathic medical student who had spent time in my office. Unfortunately, I was unable to do the same for my son, since I was not a graduate of his medical school - a local rule.

Every year I received dozens of invitations to high school and college graduations, or attendant parties. It seemed like I had just done a kindergarten exam on these students. Like Mayor Menino of Boston, who is invited to three Christmas tree lightings per evening every December, I had to say no most of the time.

I have always considered weddings to be very special, and Wendy and I were invited to far more than our share. These unions involved patients, ex-patients, parents who had become single, nurses, employees and the occasional partner. We even married off all three of our sons.

One time Wendy had just returned from a cross-country trip to see her parents. We were late for the wedding reception of a nurse at the hospital. It was August, a hundred degrees outside and twenty more inside. A doctor and his wife will always be the guests of honor at patient or nurse wedding, no matter how hard they try to meld into the background. The beaming bride led us into the sweltering kitchen. Sweat soaked through my suit, and a tall glass of iced tea would have been just fine for dinner.

The couple had saved us a plate of roast beef with a

grapefruit sized portion of mashed potatoes and gravy. It seemed as if the whole wedding party wished to sit in the kitchen and watch us eat up. I don't think doggy bags were yet in vogue, so were urged to honor the clean plate club. We were astounded by the concern of the hosts.

Another time Wendy and I were asked to attend the farm wedding of a teenager who we had helped with a number of problems at school and at home. They probably remembered me more for that fact that I had shattered her bed during a house call so many years ago. It started to sprinkle and the ceremony was moved into the barn, which was decorated with brown paper and canned goods. The whole scene was touching. Again, we were the first to enter the receiving line.

Our own wedding took place in Ottawa during Canadian Thanksgiving week. I was mostly concerned about stepping into a ripe pumpkin, as various fall vegetables had been decoratively strewn across the front of the church. I also had my groomsmen convinced that the brilliant ceremonial bunting adorning the stone facade of the Chateau Laurier was in honor of our marriage. Actually, the Queen was arriving the next day.

The inevitable flip side of all of this is that I attended my share of funerals and wakes. Wendy says we have touched all the funeral homes and many of the churches in our area at least once- sometimes she has had to go alone. Often the caskets are open - always difficult with a childhood death. Some of the intensive care staff from the medical center will always show up at wakes or funerals of mutual patients. I stood in line for forty-five

247

minutes once, at the wake of a year old infant with severe birth defects. Her RN mother had done an outstanding job of home care. Friends, neighbors, and medical personnel wanted to make certain that mother's efforts were publicly honored.

Pediatricians will often try to attend services when their former patients die as young adults. Tearful parents are often astonished to find themselves being hugged by their child's baby doctor.

No funeral was as evocative as that of Marcy, a woman with Down syndrome who died young. Her parents are lovely and courageous Mainers, and her brother played the bagpipes at the service. Wendy and I laughed and cried with all of them, and were sent home with two bottles of home-brewed cranberry wine.

LESSONS FROM ROGER

Wendy and I were visiting Montreal, where Wendy graduated from nursing school at McGill many years ago. We discovered the restaurant where she and her classmates had dined every month after saving their pennies. It had relocated several times but was still called La Caveau. You can no longer get a meal for five dollars, but our entrees that evening were excellent.

We had not seen the city in a while, so we decided to take a bus tour. The day was humid and heavy. As we boarded the bus, it became evident that the air conditioning was either turned off or broken. As the temperature soared, the patrons became increasingly agitated. The driver introduced himself as Roger and explained, in excellent English, that we would be leaving shortly.

I had noticed earlier that there were LED monitors in the Metro announcing an air quality warning. Because of its northern latitude, I had always assumed that Montreal was blessed with pristine air. In fact, the city is subject to the same cumulative automobile and power plant emissions as many Eastern cities. We later guessed that because of poor air quality, Roger was under city orders not to idle his bus.

Finally, we were off. Roger established by show of hands that we were all Yanks. For the next three hours, he wove a gentle political and moral homily intertwined with an excellent historic and geographic tour of the city. We slowly meandered through the narrow streets of Chinatown, and then past the Notre Dame Basilica chapel where Celine Dion's son would be soon baptized.

"We have very strict laws about garbage and dog poop," pronounced Roger. "There are heavy fines for those who ignore these rules. Also, this bus must pass inspection every six months. If I fail to do this, the police will come and remove the license plates the very next day. You can count on it. This is as it should be. You are a very special cargo."

We passed groups of children in the parks, streets, and metro, all sporting identically colored chapeaus and Tees. They were participating in summer recreational programs, which cost a dollar a day. Their color indicated the group's home location. When holding hands for safety they formed long undulating lines. "This is an excellent, affordable program run by the city," boasted Roger.

The bus climbed upward into Parc Mont Royal. "The concessions are licensed by the city," explained Roger. "All of the profits are returned for park maintenance."

"If we are lucky," he continued, "we may see the famous two-worker Montreal street hole. One man digging the hole and his coworker guarding it." We were fortunate. Several blocks later, we spotted this very attraction. Roger seemed pleased.

Roger also made comments about elections and retirement. Campaigns are short with regulated and transparent contributions. He pointed out that his father retired with four pensions. This was not quadruple dipping in the usual sense. The monies came separately from the government, his final employer, the military and school board job. Each fund was modest but had been invested in conservative bonds and government securities. Together they provided a comfortable retirement. No privatization. No Enron or Madoff.

Roger went into great detail about the provincial single-payer health system. There were some problems with waiting times but the plan had served his family well. A guy several rows back had finally heard enough. "That's socialism!" he wailed.

"Remember," Roger quickly retorted. "A society will ultimately be judged on how they care for their young and their old. The elderly have created the present for you and the children look to you for their future. You must remember this."

We had lunch at the St. Joseph Oratory, with a spectacular view of the city below. It reminded me of a song honoring the French who had immigrated to Maine to work in the mills and how church, work, and family were paramount in their lives. Roger continued to offer tidbits of Montreal history.

We circled back into the central city by mid-afternoon. Roger thanked us for our attention and questions about his city. He then asked us, "Which is the best city in the world?"

The passengers groaned.

"No", laughed Roger. "It is not necessarily Montreal.

251

You should feel that the best is your own hometown. When you get back, think about what I have said today. There may be a few ideas that would make your city or town a better place. Thank you again and have a good holiday."

LONG DISTANCE PLEASE

Through the miracle of modern communications technology, rural doctors are able to obtain consultations from medical specialists many miles distant. Some cases involve critically ill patients. Other children, in large sparsely populated states with few psychiatrists, can receive mental health advice via videoconferencing.

Even before these advancements, parents and even patients would ask you to make long distance phone diagnoses and suggest treatments. Often I would try.

Patients who did not flee my practice at the first hint of puberty would often stick with me until age twenty-one. Or sometimes they forgot to leave and the midnight phone call would arrive. Elizabeth was apologetic. She hadn't seen me in five years, did not have a new doctor, was on her honeymoon in Barbados, and needed an antibiotic for her bladder infection.

I have received an astonishing number of calls from institutions of higher learning. They are generally farcical.

"Hey, Dr. Moore. I know it's Sunday but since you called me back I figured you must be on call. You know I'm up here at Pine Tree U. I had a fever yesterday so I went to the infirmary and saw the nurse practitioner. She said I had X and gave me a prescription for Y. I didn't trust them so I didn't get the prescription filled."

"Why?"

"Well, Dr. Moore, my roommate says the university health service sucks."

"Does your roommate have some medical background?"

"No, Dr. Moore. He's an English major."

"What would you like me to do?"

"I think I may have a rash. I took a picture with my cell phone and e-mailed it to you. You should have gotten it by now and so can make a diagnosis, Dr. Moore. Did you get it?"

"Yes, I did, and no, I won't."

"OK. Here's what you need to do, Dr. Moore. My mom is on her way up now. I trust you. We'll meet you at your office at six thirty. Thanks a lot. You may have to write me an excuse for my mid-terms coming up next week."

One mother called me from Phoenix. Her son had a swollen red eye and high fever.

"I went to a walk-in clinic, Dr. Moore. They weren't really sure but they gave me some eye ointment. Is that OK?"

"Not really, Mrs. Smith. Where is the phone booth that you are calling from?"

Since my mum lived in Phoenix, I knew Mrs. Smith's location.

"OK. Look down the street. There is a big hospital sign. OK? Now take Jonathan down to their ER. Tell them you talked to your pediatrician back in Maine. They will know immediately that Jonathan needs to go into the hospital for intravenous antibiotics. If they don't do that, call me from the ER."

They did and Jonathan recovered from his potentially fatal eyeball infection.

Some parents refused to leave the practice when they moved. I hear the same from pediatricians around the country. One state trooper was reassigned an hour and forty-five minutes north. He wished to keep the children in my practice. I envisioned him expediting his commutes with the blue flashing lights on. I talked him into obtaining the services of a local physician. Another mother moved to the lake district in central New Hampshire. She remained in the practice. Her mother, however, still remained in our town so that the hour and a half trip to see Dr. Moore was always an outing to see Grammy. So far, even my most loyal families have honored my retirement.

The advent of the portable phone has expanded my diagnostic and therapeutic range even farther. Those older readers will recall that the first mobile phones were the size of a toaster oven. I took my first model to a high school football game I was covering. Many of the subs left the bench and wanted to make a call. This item would have never cleared airport security.

"Hey, Dr. Moore, this is Mike."

"Where are you, Mr. Mike?" Mr. Mike is a friend and my handyman. He is also a part time tugboat cook.

"I'm on the Mississippi River. I have question. How do you remove metal suture clips from the scalp? I have a mate who needs them out. Can you hear me?"

"Just barely. Can you get to shore?"

"No, we're pulling a string of barges. We don't stop that well."

"OK, you're handy. Get a needle nose pliers under the suture. Then crimp and pull."

Ten minutes pass. My phone rings again.

"Good advice. Came right out. Thanks."

"Slick as goose poop," my son would say.

A LITTLE HELP FROM MY FRIENDS

Physicians have a well-deserved reputation for arrogance. But often we need help.

Arriving back home from a day at the Air Force clinic, I told Wendy about the strange case of a child who was having periodic episodes of disorientation and slurred speech. I had no idea what was wrong with him.

"Sounds to me like he's been inhaling model airplane glue fumes in a closed area", offered my wife.

She was correct, as usual. Over the years Wendy has steered me towards several obscure diagnoses. She was especially tuned in to poisoning by the heavy metal thallium, found in rat bait. She had seen a whole family become ill by this stuff in Boston.

It took only the first day of my internship to realize that the nurses knew substantially more about medicine than I did. I stuck to them like Velcro for the entire year.

"Well, Dr. Moore, this certainly looks like congestive heart failure and not asthma. You will want to be careful and restrict fluids. I know you will want to start digitalis and a diuretic. I've figured out the doses, just sign the order sheet."

"Yes, nurse. Thank you for bringing it to my attention."

Over time I added lab techs, medical students and residents, secretaries, mothers, and hairdressers to my list of the smart and savvy. They correctly diagnosed a ruptured appendix, a bowel obstruction, a brain bleed, a rare form of pneumonia, acute leukemia, and a pituitary tumor causing diabetes. In all but the last case, I had missed the diagnosis.

Twice in the last decade mothers and grandmothers have diagnosed blindness and less severe vision problems in their young charges. But sometimes grandmothers may an impediment to healing. Many years ago, the late Dr. Sydney Gellis, a national pediatric icon from Boston, described a number of instances where a misguided granny removed her hospitalized grandchild's tracheotomy tube, feeding tube or IV because the device was "hurting" the youngster. Fortunately, I have never encountered this problem firsthand. The grandparents in my practice brought their grandchildren in for office visits and made diagnoses. I salute them. They are treasures.

A few years ago my son's partner in their Western state was caring for a child with Q fever. Q fever was first seen in the areas of Australia where cattle are raised. It is caused by a small bacterium similar to the one that causes Legionnaires disease. Veterinarians, meat handlers, and sheep shearers are at risk. It is a very rare disease but one bacterium can start a fatal chain of event. I started to compliment his partner on making this very difficult diagnosis.

"Actually," my son confessed",My partner didn't make the diagnosis. The next door neighbor did. He wanted to make certain his friend's sick son didn't have that disease with the funny name that you get from skinning rabbits."

One night in the emergency room, I was stumped by a suddenly mute girl. The on-call social worker suggested that mother take the child to the mall and have a heart to heart over lunch. Unfortunately the mental health professional was spot on. The child later tearfully acknowledged sexual abuse by her father.

Occasionally, I am one dispensing unsolicited advice. Just after my arrival in Maine, I was in the hospital late one night and was able to help resuscitate an elderly patient. The next day the other doctor, a surgeon who was the chief of staff, stopped me in the corridor.

"Thank you for your help with the cardiac arrest last night, Dr. Moore."

"Anytime," I replied, immediately regretting my words. "Actually, sir, I'm sure there won't be another time."

I was visiting my pediatrician son. He was unable to leave a sick preemie and walk the two blocks to his home for Sunday breakfast. I offered to bring some food to the nursery. When I arrived he was about to place a catheter into the baby's umbilical artery which was sitting in the umbilical stump. A ventilator was breathing for the baby. The eggs would have to wait. My mother-in-law taught me to be useful and not just stand around if things needed to be done. I offered to help. "Sure," he agreed.

The nurses soon had me gowned and gloved. The catheter would allow us to follow the infant's arterial oxygen and acid level, which are mandatory signals for a baby on a breathing machine. Threading plastic tubing into an umbilical artery is akin to pushing a cooked piece of spaghetti through a hollow swizzle stick. There are tools to help.

Suddenly I realized that I had no hospital privileges to be doing this. I knew my own hospital by-laws had a provision for deputizing out-of-town doctors during emergencies and natural disasters. Once I had rushed a sick toddler to the medical center via ambulance. On the ward I was informed that the pediatric surgeon and all the residents were elsewhere attending to emergencies. My patient needed a new IV and some other treatments. It was just me and the medical student. I had no formal privileges at the center. When I addressed the nurse, she smiled and shrugged. Onward we went.

Was this the same? Would the nurses tell? I was reassured when a one of them took our picture. I had the photo framed and it remains one of my favorites.

Our first attempt was a bust, but that's the reason babies have two umbilical arteries, as well as eyes, kidneys, ovaries and all the rest. The second attempt went better and the baby stabilized.

Since our third son, David has Masters Degrees in Religion and Ethics, this chapter seems to be the only appropriate space for a quick thank you. After being awarded the above, David now claimed he had "more useless degrees than a broken thermometer". It was time to go to work to spend time with several nonprofits – always with humanitarian missions.

Once, after summiting Mt. Lafayette in New Hampshire with David on one of my significant birthdays, I magically produced cans of semi-frozen beer and bourbon/ginger ale from deep in my daypack.

"Whew," he exclaimed in relief. "I saw them in the freezer last night and thought you had become a closet drinker."

Another time, David and I built a loft bed for his basement dorm room at Colby College. Working with only plans in my head, I purchased excessive lumber for the project. On a brilliant fall day, we assembled the beast on the lawn outside – accepting advice from passer-by students and parents. The item began to look like Noah's Ark. We then had to disassemble the unit and reassemble it in the dorm room. It filled the whole space. At the end of the year, David chose the upside down foreclosure plan, twenty years before its time, and just walked away.

I have leaned on David for ethics advice on a number of occasions. The answer was either – "I wouldn't do that" or "You know that's OK – you didn't need to call".

Lastly, David is truly a renaissance man. He and his buddy are probably the only tourist pair that have ever visited the separate Kentucky gravesites of Catholic theologian Thomas Merton AND Elvis in the same twenty-four hour span. Thank you.

SECURITY SAGAS

We doctors often view the angels and ourselves above God, but in the grand scheme of things, we lack authority.

Living in a border state with a Canadian wife, I have had far more than my share of encounters with customs agents. Early in our marriage, we would share the driving on long trips, but Wendy would always take the wheel whenever we approached the border. This was for two reasons. First, my French is horrible. Second, I always foolishly said that we had nothing to declare, which generally led to a request to "please pull over and pop the trunk". Wendy's answer, that we were bringing brownies, cider, and a few gifts worth under a hundred dollars, was always greeted with a smile and wave-through by the agent. One time our auto was searched up one side and down the other, after which the authorities were effusively apologetic, explaining that we had won their random full- inspection lottery.

There have been other glitches at the Canadian border. Once, confused while motoring across a remote Vermont crossing, I triggered a wailing siren by failing to recognize that the customs office was in fact part of a general store. Another time, at a similarly rural crossing, a stern agent grilled me as to exactly what kind of job I had in southern Maine after watching Wendy and I switch seats. We were probably the first car through in several hours.

One morning at the Denver International Airport, I handed my passport to a friendly lady from the

Transportation Security Authority.

A purple beam flashed as she scanned the document. The agent squinted and scanned my passport once again. The crowd noise suddenly quieted as she spoke.

"What kind of a doctor are you?"

"Pediatrician," I whispered.

"Well, doctor."

I had already imagined my body search in the adjacent room. Would they laugh at my new green and red Grinch boxer shorts? I was fairly certain my back pain pills were in a properly labeled bottle from the pharmacy. I would miss my flight and would have to sleep on an airport bench. The official paused again and looked me straight in the eye.

"Well, doctor . . . thank you for taking care of our children. Have a safe flight."

Many years ago, I was enjoying a quiet evening in the home of Reverend Noel in Terrier Rouge, Haiti. We were playing and singing with some local children.

A loud knock rattled the wooden front door. The pastor opened the door to reveal two armed uniformed custom agents holding a lantern.

Earlier in the day Jimmy, Laura and I had visited the Citadelle. This historic mountaintop castle was built by hand around 1800 with huge cannons designed to thwart Napoleon's return to the island. The guns were never fired. With the guide's lukewarm approval, Jimmy had removed a cannonball for his collection of military artifacts in Maine.

"Is the doctor here?" The larger agent demanded.

"Jimmy!" I whispered. "They know about the cannon-ball."

I immediately envisioned both of us languishing for years in a Haitian jail while the community rallied for our release.

I raised my hand and then noticed that other agent was cradling an infant.

"I need the doctor to examine my son."

I took a deep breath and smelled the sweet tropical air. It turned out that the child had a birth defect and needed follow-up care. At the father's request, I sent him a letter on my office stationary officially requesting a consultation at Miami Children's Hospital. I never found out if this occurred. Government officials are often reluctant to have natives leave the island for medical evaluations. They often don't return.

I remember a time in the 1960's when I volunteered to staff an Air Force ambulance along the parade route at Lyndon Johnson's inauguration. We were parked on a side street half a block off Pennsylvania Avenue. Our tight little unit featured a driver, a medic, a very large military policeman, and me. The President was due in thirty minutes. Suddenly, I watched in astonishment as two men dressed in farm clothes sauntered down the street towards the parade route. They both carried shotguns, and they were joking with each other as if they were sitting on the front porch.

I tapped our cop on the shoulder and pointed. The next sixty seconds are a blur, as the MP became airborne and police descended from rooftops and unmarked cars. The two pedestrians disappeared in an instant.

"What was that?" I gasped.

"I have no idea," said the medic and driver in unison.

The mystery was solved the next day when the full story appeared in the Washington newspapers. Apparently, the pair were Virginia farmers, walking back to the bus station after getting their guns serviced at a local shop. Fortunately, for everyone, they were not carrying any ammunition. The police gave them lunch at the station, let them watch the festivities on TV, and brought them back to the bus station.

Since our town is just down the road from the Bush family compound, I have occasionally run into President George H.W. Bush and his wife Barbara. His presence in retail stores is always heralded by serious-looking men in dark business suits with wires hanging out of their ears. Once, while running a marathon with my eyes riveted on the yellow line at mile ten, I practically bumped into the fender of his limousine. On another occasion, a military chopper dropped into the hospital parking lot, just feet above me as I exited the office. It was testing out the air space between us and Walker's Point.

One summer Sunday, I decided to forgo my local church and headed for St. Ann's Church in Kennebunkport. Rev. Billy Graham and his wife were houseguests at the Bush's and he would give the sermon at this stone chapel by the sea. As usual, I was a few minutes late, arriving just as the service began. There were no seats left, so I crouched under an open window in an attempt to hear the homily. I picked up an occasional reference to saints and prophets but was unable to follow the theme.

Suddenly I was aware of two men in dark suits pressing in close. I thought of letters from lawyers and state police, the books smuggled into Russia, and parking in the General's space. Was I in trouble yet again? I'll never know for sure, but the Secret Service acted like they just wanted to chitchat during the service. They remained vigilant the whole time.

Finally, the service ended and the doors opened. Looking around, Reverend Graham spotted the dozen of us who had been standing outside and, to my amazement, invited our group to sit with him on some stone benches nearby that overlooked the ocean. The view was a shimmering collage of sailboats and lobster pots.

He spent the next twenty minutes telling us about his meetings with various world leaders - from Africa to the Kremlin, China to South America. The stories were intimate and fascinating, with an ecumenical tone.

267

At the end, we all shook his hand and thanked him warmly. A friendly and well-dressed woman stood next to me. Normally I might have whined about sweating in the sun for an hour. But Dr. Graham's thoughtfulness and grace had put me on a different level.

"Dr. Graham didn't have to do that. He is a very impressive gentleman," I said to her.

"I think so too," responded the lady.

Several moments later, a bystander asked, "What was Mrs. Graham talking to you about?"

IT SHOULDN'T HURT TO BE A CHILD

It was a hot morning in July 2003. As usual, I brought Wendy a pot of tea and the morning paper in bed. "Oh, Conner," she winced, pointing to a headline and a photograph.

In 1962, Dr. Henry Kemp published his explosive paper "The Battered Child Syndrome" in *The Journal of the American Medical Association.* It introduced the concept of intentional child injury. The report was the culmination of several decades of growing concern about bizarre and often unexplainable pediatric trauma, especially to young infants. Brain bleeding without a fall, long bone fractures in children too young to walk, and youngsters with sexually transmitted diseases were only a few examples. The questionable explanations given by caregivers included spontaneous brain hemorrhage, soft bones (without family history), and gonorrhea from the toilet seat.

At the time of the report, pediatricians were just beginning to establish their role as family consultants for childcare. They were generally reluctant to rock the boat by accusing families of abusing their own children. Dr. Kemp's findings hit the nation like a tidal wave and had an immediate legal impact. Over the next three years, every state passed "good Samaritan" protection for those reporting suspicious injuries and imposed penalties for failing to do so. A national child abuse center was established for training and research.

A number of years ago an infant was brought to my

office at four months of age. He had sustained micro fractures of the knee and ankles, evidence of non-accidental injury. The parents denied abuse and implicated the sitter. Criminal charges were not filed. The child was placed in foster care, where he thrived. His bones healed and no new fractures developed. He was eventually reunited with his mother.

The newspaper story that my wife showed me stated that an adult with the same surname had been arrested in a small town, four months after his infant son was found dead in his crib, supposedly from sudden infant death syndrome. But, during interrogation, his wife confessed to viewing her husband place a pillow over his crying son's face. Detectives then discovered that the suspect had another son who had died of SIDS four years earlier in an adjacent state, and ten years prior had four children removed from his home. We not only prevented further injury to the infant, but may have saved his life.

Even with mandatory reporting, the diagnosis of child abuse is treacherous territory. Every time I think I'm reasonably skilled in this area, I am late in a diagnosis. Especially in the era before computed tomography scans, non-incidental brain injury was often silent until damage had been done. A spinal tap yields unexpectedly bloody fluid. A seizing child has an area of retinal hemorrhage– evidence of shaken baby syndrome.

Reporting child abuse is an emotionally charged event for everyone involved. I attempt to explain that I am mandated by law to notify authorities of suspicious injuries. My job is to make certain that such a child is in a protected environment, not to determine who is responsible for the trauma. That task rests with the police and social services, and sometimes a jury. Civil suits for missed battering have been successfully litigated against doctors after the injured child turns eighteen.

It can be very difficult. I do have families in the practice with proven brittle bone problems. Their babies sometimes have fractures at birth. Toddlers can break legs falling off couches and down stairs. Abusive parents were frequently abused as children.

Public education can go a long way towards preventing child abuse. A local program, started after the death of a shaken baby, educates caregivers about this devastating syndrome. Mandatory reporting has proven invaluable. An exciting program has been instituted in at least one European country. There, visiting nurses make frequent visits to the homes of all babies after they leave the nursery. They do not snoop for abuse, but make a general assessment of the home situation and serve as a friendly consultant for childcare questions. Studies show a significant decrease in damaged children. This can be a chapter with a happy ending.

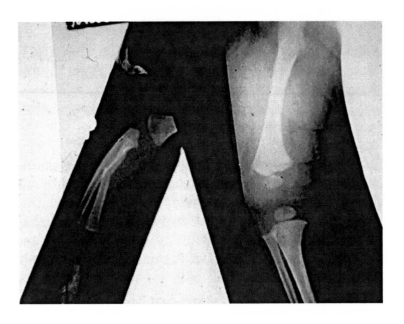

Pictured: non accidental child injury x-ray

A WEIGHTY PROBLEM

The 1950s were not as healthy and wholesome as popular culture would have you believe. Teens drank their share of alcohol and cigarettes were ubiquitous across every segment of society. Polio, measles, and meningitis were still a threat, and seat belts were an exotic luxury. But kids were leaner and more fit. In junior high, I was a cashier at the cafeteria, a silent observer of school lunch nutrition. These meals were often bland but they were always healthy – meat, chicken or fish with a side of vegetables. There were no cheeseburgers, fried chicken nuggets, or soft drinks on the menu. Pizza had barely made a dent in American culinary consciousness. I would estimate that each tray held no more than five or six hundred calories.

I biked or walked to school, about two miles each way. When we got there, physical education was mandatory. Fast food was not easily available and could be risky. White Castle was the only such restaurant in the county. I was always leery of snack food after my friend Steve bit into a processed single-serving cherry pie and found a bright green ball of mold in the center. Snacks were for special occasions –not for daily consumption. Stay-at-home moms, smiling from behind clean white aprons, served home cooked meals every evening. After school and in the summertime, we biked everywhere. It was a short trip to our small downtown. There you could buy everything from screws for your model railroad to 45 RPM records- no five mile car trip to the big box store. Our primitive black and white TV, with its grainy and jumpy picture, caused boredom and headaches.

I recall these scenes only to document the changes that have contributed to today's national obesity epidemic. Like few other social phenomena, this problem has unfolded vividly before my eyes. A perfect storm of processed foods, working moms, readily available fast food, decentralized shopping zones, an explosion of video screens, an absence of sidewalks and trails, and unhealthy school lunches have placed both children and adults at risk for life-threatening health consequences.

Twelve million American children, one in three, are either overweight or obese. The body mass index (BMI) is an estimate of body fat. In kids the calculation is a bit more complicated. You toss the child's height and weight into a formula, mix in age and sex and out pops a percentile number. Overweight is over 85th percentile, obesity is over 95th percentile. As the BMI rises, risk for medical problems will follow like a shadow.

The silent epidemic of obesity has the potential for crippling our already fragile health care system. The siren will sound with marked increases in type II diabetes, heart attacks, hypertension, fatty livers and strokes. Obesity is also correlated to asthma and depression. Overweight children are subject to discrimination in academics, sports and social situations – and later with dating and jobs. They are frequently bullied and low self esteem is common.

If this trend of increasing obesity continues, there will simply not be enough medical personnel to treat the overweight. That sounds harsh but I believe it to be true. If the numbers of annual premature deaths caused by obesity were instead blamed on industrial accidents or plane crashes, the national outcry would be deafening. We are becoming numb to the issue. Even I no longer wince when examining a 150 pound third-grader.

What to do? The first step should be a regular physical with your child's physician. They can calculate BMI and determined if it has changed, check for medical problems, and recommend prevention or treatment of overweight or obesity. Moreover, these visits can identify those children with stress, depression, anxiety, anger, and boredom who use comfort food to alleviate their symptoms. Chronic obesity may cause brain changes similar to those seem with addiction; food will alleviate their mental pain and contribute to the downhill spiral. Many of the remedies involve strategies listed below.

At the national level the President and Congress can feature their own healthy lifestyles. Any money spent or redirected now to support better school lunches and fitness programs will reduce the cost of later health care. Tens of billions of dollars could be saved just on type II diabetes alone.

The states can help in a similar fashion. Abandoned rail and road beds can be converted to walking and biking trails. Awards from tobacco lawsuits should be used to promote healthy activities rather than being dumped into general state coffers. States can also support programs that foster healthy school lunches and exercise programs.

Locally, much can be accomplished. Go online to see

how Appleton, Wisconsin altered its school lunch menu and created quieter and more focused students. Many inner-city children have gone before local school boards pleading for the removal of fatty, salty junk food from the school cafeterias. This is a no-brainer, to which students will quickly adapt. Several teachers in my city have reported calmer students when vending machines were removed from their school. Many towns are actively involved in creating walking and biking trails – some designing safe venues to and from school.

Most importantly, parents need to set examples. Children will not buy into lifestyle changes unless the whole family is on board. A starting point is the 5210 reminder - 5 daily serving of fruits/veggies, maximum 2 hours TV, 1 hour exercise, and zero sugary drinks. Family home dinners, less eating out, no TV in the bedroom, decreased consumption of white foods, and participation in school sports are just a few other preventative suggestions.

If we had a pill that would make you feel better, become slimmer, and prevent a host of chronic diseases, citizens would be breaking down pharmacy doors to obtain this wonder drug. A proper diet and a bit of exercise can provide these benefits now.

THE GREAT OUTDOORS

"You are so lucky to be living in Maine."

This well-intentioned sentence is often uttered by hikers from away. They have saved their pennies to spend a week or two exploring the Maine wilderness or seacoast. Well outfitted, these seasonal hikers look to me for an answer to their implied question. My choice of home location was a carefully calculated compromise between the ocean vote of my navy brat wife and my ballot for the mountains.

It was not luck that our family arrived in Maine and these summer warriors could have made a similar choice. Although I was raised in the New York suburbs, my father's home was in northwest Iowa and my mother hailed from Wisconsin. My choice to attend college in northern New Hampshire was probably an unconscious attempt to flee to a greener environment.

Oddly, the green outdoors might have nudged me down the pre-med path. It was college spring weekend. We chemistry majors were cloistered in a dank fourth floor lab wrestling the dreaded quant-qual exam. Given a teaspoon of unknown powder, it was our job to not only separate and identify the compound, but to also report its weight. Below, a brilliant New England spring day held court as couples walked hand in hand clutching six-packs of beer. Everything seemed vibrantly verdant.

As the afternoon droned on, weird odors and strong invective filled the lab. After six hours, I presented my orange powder results to the teaching assistant. I had nailed the name but botched weight- yielding a firm C. I shuffled back to my lab bench and gazed out the window again. " This is madness," I mumbled - echoing words uttered by Colonel Nicholson as his own countrymen exploded his POW -built *Bridge over the River Kwai.* This epiphany led me away from a future amidst plumes of chemical acids towards the pristine coast of Maine. My career change was further encouraged by a summer job tallying marketing surveys in a New York ad agency; would a housewife buy coffee because of FLAVOR or AROMA? Maybe I could do better.

Despite summer New England mountain climbing during med schools breaks, I soon returned to seven years of urban medical training and military service - with marriage and the birth of a child in the middle. The turmoil of the cities in the 60s probably set the table for a move to a quieter setting.

My back to- the -land yearning may have been ingrained on some obscure chromosome. We now know there are similar gene foci for traits such as shyness and risk taking behavior. Wendy also had spent part of her childhood in rural Nova Scotia. My father's family had left Vermont in the late 1800s for the economic promise of Midwestern farmland.

There are few locations in the East where the mountains approach the sea. You can travel from my costal home in Maine to Shawnee Peak, with respectable downhill skiing and hiking, in a little over an hour. From this summit, with binoculars on a clear day, one can see the weather station and possibly black smoke from the cog railway engine atop Mt. Washington thirty miles away. You can also quickly climb up the Camden Hills if you live along the southwestern edge of Penobscot Bay. You might do almost the same in New Hampshire but the coast is crowded and traffic congested. That is it for the east coast. Period. That is why I'm here. The fact that my children can go trout fishing in a city where moose, bear, and coyotes have been observed is a bonus.

What are the benefits of the great outdoors? A few days or a week in the mountains or on an ocean island is worth at least half dozen visits to your therapist- and significantly cheaper. You will also meet some wonderful outdoors persons from both in state and away. If you hike solo, there are several peaks where, especially off-season, you can have lunch, lay back and enjoy the absolute, absolute silence. My favorites are a secret. Then for dessert, you might be able to view a red-tailed hawk, turkey vulture, or bald eagle through your binoculars.

Recently, there has been much written about the outdoor deprivation syndrome. The British Good Child Inquiry has chronicled the migration of children from the great outdoors towards ever-beckoning video and computer screens leading to a consumer mind-set at an ever-decreasing age. When the demand for expensive consumer goods goes unfulfilled, the child or teen often becomes angry or depressed. In my chapter on cars, my friend Tony from California states that on the west coast, "you are what you drive." Some children, after countless hours of media exposure, are a product of their environment. The English study had enough observations and recommendation to fill a hefty book.

Concern for safety and public apathy towards outdoor programs and playgrounds are problematic. On brilliant fall mornings, I have witnessed schoolchildren hermetically sealed inside cars, while waiting for school busses. It may be that bullying or fear of abduction was involved- that would be a shame. The role of outdoor time in reducing obesity, type II diabetes, smoking, drug use, and mental health disorders has been documented.

Introduce your children to day hikes at an early age. Every region, both here and across the nation, has its own supply of guidebooks to local day trips. Walking trails, often using abandoned railroad spurs or trolley lines, are being developed all across our state and nation. If children get involved early, they will keep hiking. We need to reduce the downward trend of park usage- the curve should be upward.

NEVER GIVE UP

I had only been retired for a week when my son Michael, a decent golfer, called me up and said "I've been waiting for this. You're my new caddie." I agreed to support him in his quest to qualify for the Maine Amateur and asked him what this would entail. "Just follow Jack Nicklaus's rules for caddies", he joked. "Show up, keep up, and shut up". As it turns out, we have had moderate success as team, and our time together on the course has been one of the highlights of my retirement.

Our first attempt to qualify was at Sanford in 2008. Michael was going along pretty well until he blasted his tee shot on the twelfth hole deep into the woods. In this case, the golfer and his caddie are allotted five minutes to conduct a search and rescue mission for the wayward ball. We were approaching this limit when I saw a ball in the darkness. I got right down on my hands and knees, and put my aging eyes about three inches from it.

"Titleist?"

"Don't touch it!"

"Number six?"

"Don't touch anything near it! Get up!"

It was not to be our day. The next year the qualifier was at the Biddeford-Saco Country Club, a mile from my house. Michael came down the night before, and we arrived at the course well rested and in good spirits. He nearly aced the second hole, tapping in for birdie, and was off and running. In the twelfth fairway he leaned over to me and said, "We got a pretty good round going."

"I know", I answered. "I didn't want to say anything."

The golfing gods do not take kindly to this sort of hubris. Disaster struck on the fourteenth. From 130 yards away, dead in the middle of the fairway, Michael took *eight* more shots to get down, gave up five strokes to par, and just about eliminated himself. I must admit that my thoughts turned towards lunch.

Michael hit last on the next hole, a difficult par-three. He purred an eight iron, which covered the flag as it disappeared behind a mound in front of the green. One of our fellow competitors raced ahead in his cart, peered into the hole, and raised both arms. Michael had canned his second career hole-in-one. He played the last three holes carefully and qualified for the Maine Amateur on his fifth attempt.

That was a trivial example by a proud father, but my point is clear. Persistence and positive thinking can make a huge difference when confronting a serious illness or injury. Winston Churchill said it most forcefully in his famous speech to the students at Harrow School in October 1941 after ten months of Nazi blitz bombing, "never give up, never give up, never, never, never..."

My first major challenge after arriving in Maine was baby Robert. He arrived a few weeks early and required every ounce of my attention. I could see the nurses sizing me up. Robert would be my informal state license test and pediatric board test, all in one. There was neither an intensive care unit at the medical center nor ventilators at our local hospital. I was the intern, resident and attending physician. Robert had respiratory distress, jaundice, infection, and a host of other problems. Every few hours, I would trot back up to the hospital. My mother had just arrived to help with my second son's impending birth, and she was horrified at the amount of time I spent away from my family.

The nurses were very skilled and they were the prime reason for Robert's survival. We exchanged his blood, treated his infection, and breathed for him when he forgot to. Robert's skin became tight like candle wax from a condition called sclerema, which I had seen only once before. We treated it with steroids. Gradually we won each battle and finally the war. Robert was a bit below average in school. However, he never developed cerebral palsy or any other motor problems.

A few months later, a call came from the emergency room. A young infant was having some respiratory distress. The wheezing baby's chest was full of something. A chest x-ray showed spotty dark areas, possibly from aspirated food or saliva.

"Dr. Moore. Every time I feed the baby she turns blue and coughs."

This is a fairly common complaint, I suspected reflux and asked the mother to thicken the formula and administer it more slowly. This was not much help. The

283

infant slowly gained weight but her symptoms persisted. Chest x-ray still showed a few patchy areas in the lung.

I started to worry about a T-E fistula, a conflation of the windpipe and the esophagus. Both of these tubes start out as a single tube in the fetus. They then separate, but sometimes not completely. In the common type of T-E fistula, the esophagus ends in a blind pouch and never reaches the stomach. All the breast milk or formula immediately winds up in the lungs. In another manifestation, the windpipe and esophagus develop normally except for a tiny hole that connects them. A little bit of each feeding gets squirted into the windpipe, with long-term consequences.

I sent the baby into the medical center and asked them to consider this diagnosis. At that time, our tools were crude. The specialist placed purple dye into the esophagus and could not see any stains in the windpipe.

The baby gained weight slowly. The family moved to New Hampshire. We transferred records and arranged for close follow-up. A year later, a call came from the emergency room.

I went down to examine the infant. I gasped as I saw the struggling toddler who was breathing like an eighty-year-old smoker. I knew that we missed the diagnosis. I sent the infant back to our medical center. Never give up.

This time, better imaging techniques revealed the sought-after connection between the esophagus and windpipe. The toddler was indeed feeding his lung as well as his stomach each time he swallowed. The fistula was surgically tied off and I assume the child did well.

I remember two other children who never gave up. Barbara had rheumatoid arthritis, a very nasty condition in children. Beyond aspirin, cortisone and a few leukemia drugs, we had no good tools for this painful disease. Driving through a snowstorm to the hospital one morning, I glimpsed Barbara through the windshield wipers. She was limping up the stairs to junior high school to maintain her perfect attendance record.

Jonathan was born with defects in his lower spine. His right leg was short. He had bowel and bladder problems. He needed a colostomy bag and a draining tube from his bladder. Despite his severe disabilities, he grew and thrived. The family moved away and later returned. I followed this courageous child through numerous surgeries and problems at school. His father moved many miles north but still brought his son to see me. I particularly remember one day when I was grumbling about my back or maybe a cold. The examining room door flew open and there was Jonathan – crutches, tubes, and ear-to-ear smile. Then in a loud voice he asked, "Hey, Dr. Moore. How are you? Havin' a good day?"

OVER AND OUT

As a prelude to writing this book, I read a number of autobiographies by doctors, focusing on those by pediatricians and rural practitioners. Many were angry and extremely frustrated at the current state of medicine and society in general. I prefer to remember an episode related to me by one of Wendy's cousins. He was standing on the deck of a British carrier towards the end of World War II. Suddenly, a kamikaze plane dove at the vessel. He and some fellow sailors sprinted down a stairwell. The other half tried to escape in a different direction and were all killed instantly. Since that time Wendy's relative vowed to never dance with the emotions of fear, anger or jealously. "They really are not productive and life is very short," he explained.

I tried to view my forty years as being a time when I was given the privilege to care for sick children. As a neighbor once stated, "I trust you with my most cherished possession – my child." On occasion I may have failed, but not for a lack of effort.

I was blessed with professors and instructors who were magnificent teachers, at the lectern and bedside. They drilled into me honesty, the importance of continuing education, and a keen awareness that serious disease generally arrives at night and on the weekend. Wendy would often push me out of bed after a 3 AM phone call from the emergency room. "You have no idea what's wrong with that child. Go! I won't be able to go back to sleep until you leave." A senior partner reminded me to "never refuse" to see a sick child regardless of the family's ability to pay.

287

My chief gave me some sage advice as I left my training. He urged me to periodically spend time at some nearby teaching hospital – perhaps trading the teaching of students and residents for time in a specialty clinic of my choice. I attempted to do that, especially with the care of newborns. I liberally sprinkled the office with visiting medical students and residents. The teaching roster gradually expanded to encompass aspiring nurse practitioners, physician's assistants, nurses, and emergency medical technicians. There were days when my clinic looked like the yellow brick road. Our practice families embraced these groups of trainees.

A retiring surgeon once counseled his fellow doctors to be on good terms with their families - six months after they left the hospital, nobody would remember them. He also said that, during practice years, they might consider the purchase of a small getaway camp or cabin. Over the years, it would be far less costly than a psychiatrist.

One of my few credos is to avoid giving unsolicited advice. Nevertheless, the Academy of Pediatrics strongly urges me to comment in the office on your chubby or scholastically underachieving child, even if you didn't bring up the subject. Perhaps a few thoughts might be of value.

As a parent, be aware of your actions. Your offspring, as you well know, come equipped with laser memories. Years later, they will recall your dining table talk – the good stuff, such as praising a friend and the bad, as in boasting of tax evasion. Spend time with your children. Show up, sometimes unannounced, at their sporting

288

events and concerts.

Encourage spontaneous family walks and hikes – sometimes including local buddies. I remember once leading a group of neighborhood children into northern Baxter State Park. It was true bear country. One fast-flowing stream cascaded straight downward into a jumble of chutes and caverns. It looked like a water theme park. The group took great glee in sending me down solo to test the safety of the tortuous route. I emerged after what seemed like an eternity, with frigid, but pristine, water pouring out of my nose and mouth. From a distance, high above I could hear a small child announce "It's OK. Doc made it and he doesn't look too bad."

Children will thrive amidst both strict and more liberal parenting styles – as long as they are valued and loved. There must always be consequences if the child interferes with the rights of others, either physically or verbally. Your children should also know that in any dispute with teachers or coaches, "the ruling on the field is confirmed in the adult's favor", unless there is incontrovertible evidence to the contrary. Unfortunately, the opposite seems to prevail today.

Read to your offspring. It will foster good habits. Try to eat together as a family at least a few times a week. I know this may be difficult with two parents working and nocturnal sports practices and games. Social workers at our local children's home urge foster parents to establish family rituals around holidays and other important dates. Many of their little wanderers have never been exposed to such celebrations. My own grandchildren enjoy mid-afternoon tea and cookies. This ritual must always progress in the same order each time- with me, the eldest, being offered the first cookie.

In my nurse's room, there was a poster, which read: "one hundred years from now nobody will remember the size of your house, car, or bank account - but they will remember if you made a difference in the life of a child". I salute those parents, nurses, mental health workers, teachers and doctors who are making a difference.

One morning during my last week in practice, I walked down the driveway at five o'clock to fetch the morning paper. To the east, a magenta dawn burst from the horizon. To the west a full rainbow arched across a fading night sky. I had never witnessed that combination in the past. However, as Jessi once sagely observed, "I always feel better after seeing a rainbow."

God speed to all.

ABOUT THE AUTHOR

Picture courtesy of Thornton Academy: Dr. Moore 2006

A Board certified pediatrician since 1970, Dr. Moore was born in Detroit. He graduated from Dartmouth College in 1960 with a BA and then attended Cornell University Medical College, earning a Doctorate in Medicine in 1963.

Following an internship at Boston City Hospital from 1963-64, Dr. Moore enlisted in the USAF as a General Medical Officer assigned to Pediatrics. After two years of service, he completed his residency in pediatrics at Cincinnati Children's Hospital.

As a physician in private practice in Biddeford, Maine, Dr. Moore moved his wife Wendy and their family to neighboring Saco in 1968, where they became an active part of the community, which began his forty plus years as a pediatrician.

During his career, Dr. Moore served as a staff pediatrician at Sweetser Children's Home, Past President of the Medical Staff at Southern Maine Medical Center, School and Sports Physician at Thornton Academy in Saco and School Physician in Biddeford Maine.

Dr. Moore has been the recipient of many awards including: Caregiver of the Year Award from Southern Maine Medical Center in 2004, The Carl Pendleton Award from Sweetser Children's Home in 2005, and an Achievement Award and 35 Year Recognition Award from The American Academy of Pediatrics.

He continues to work part time and volunteers regularly at local blood drives, flu clinics, and substitutes at the Maine Medical Center Residency Program.

In his free time, Dr. Moore loves to garden, hike and spend time with his wife of 46 years, their three sons and their families.

ACKNOWLEDGEMENTS

I have already thanked my family for their support and enthusiasm. A few nurses and physicians have been cited in the book. It soon became evident that it would be impossible to name and thank the scores of health professionals who have worked days, nights, weekends and holidays to serve the children of Southern Maine. They have come to work through blizzards, gunfire, and three feet of water. They have totaled cars while driving home on icy roads. They are physicians, nurses, secretaries, lab techs, radiology techs, medical assistants, pediatric ward and OB staff, ER staff, ambulance crews, highway workers, and many other groups. If I try to name you all, I will leave out many.

I salute the courageous children with chronic illness and their equally brave parents. They endure days of painful disability, frequent doctor visits, midnight ambulance rides, and hours of tears. Watching these families will suddenly remind me of what is important in life.

Many thanks to our local hospital CEO and Board of Directors for their support of Pediatrics. This specialty has long been known as the fifth teet on the medical cow. Hospitalized children do not generate very much revenue – many are insured by Medicaid or uninsured. It would have been understandable if the Board had decided, at some point, not to support inpatient Pediatrics – but they did not. Thank you.

Gratitude goes to Lisa Tener and her writer's blog – a must for aspiring authors. Also thanks to author and book coach Kathy Rich for support and encouragement. The annual Harvard Medical Writer's Conference is a gem.

I again thank the parents and their children who have allowed me to tell their stories in this book.

Lastly, kudos to Deb Landry, my publisher, for her decision to take on this somewhat risky project. Deb has always had a passion for the well-being of children. She has been a mover and shaker in the battle to eliminate child bullying in Maine and the rest of the country. Deb has been instrumental in the establishment of a local after school theatrical program – taking kids off the street while boosting their self-esteem and academic aspirations. The list goes on. She has gently guided me through the many minefields littering the publishing pathway with patience and enthusiasm. Thank you.

Memories from Dr. Moore's photo album

Pictured: Wedding of David and Rebecca at the Chapel of the
Bells, Reno NV; August 13, 2009

Pictured below: Jessi and Dr. Moore on Halloween

1974: The Moore Family, L to R: Christopher, David, Michael, Wendy and Dr. Moore

2007: The Moore Family at David's wedding

L-R Christopher, David, Wendy, Dr. Moore, Michael

Pictured: Maine Central Railroad, approaching
Crawford Notch, NH

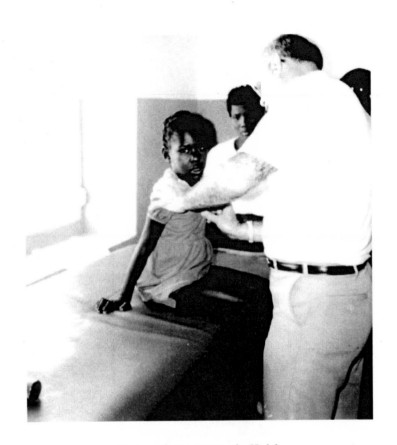

Pictured: Dr. Moore in Haiti